Cover and interior design by Kaitlyn Bitner/Ankerwycke.

In 1215, the Magna Carta was sealed underneath the ancient Ankerwycke Yew tree, starting the process that led to rule by constitutional law—in effect, giving rights and the law to the people. Today, the ABA's Ankerwycke line of books continues to bring the law to the people. With legal fiction, true crime books, popular legal histories, public policy handbooks, and prescriptive guides to current legal and business issues, Ankerwycke is a contemporary and innovative line of books for everyone from a trusted and vested authority.

Printed in the United States of America.
18 17 16 15 5 4 3 2 1

ISBN: 978-1-62722-761-2
e-ISBN: 978-1-62722-762-9

Library of Congress Cataloging-in-Publication Data

Discounts are available for books ordered in bulk. Special consideration is given to state bars, CLE programs, and other bar-related organizations. Inquire at Book Publishing, ABA Publishing, American Bar Association, 321 N. Clark Street, Chicago, Illinois 60654-7598.

www.ShopABA.org

FOREWORD

Mentors, advisors, consultants, instructors: Who wants to spend time with someone who's a drag? Which is why I was so relieved when Jeff Cohen wrote a book. A guy I knew as fast on his feet, fun, smart and engaging had decided to pass along some of what he's learned in the Hollywood trenches from being a young actor to a top attorney and savvy dealmaker. I knew it wouldn't be a dreary dry tome, and thankfully, it's just the opposite.

Jeff understands the entertainment business' rules of the road, but he's also wise to all of the rule bending and breaking that industry's regularly practice and often without breaking a sweat. Jeff gets a kick out of much of it, which makes absorbing some of tougher lessons of "The Town" perhaps less bitter and depression-inducing.

But Jeff's book would really just be a time-burner if it was only about the tenor and tone of all the zigging and zagging that occurs among the frantic herds of nervous successes and the desperate wannabes. The Jeff I've encountered around the biz and through working on *Variety's* Ten to Watch series of upcoming career profiles is extremely passionate about constantly rejuvenating our business with new creatives and execs. Advice-giving isn't a gig to sell books; it's part of Jeff's life mission, and he's energetically and resourcefully committed to it.

There is a common thread between Jeff's busy law office, his extremely proactive and creative dealmaking and his commitment to not just assisting and educating the next generation but also serving as priest, rabbi and legal eagle to the timeless dreamers and salty pros who have no age. He generously shares a lot of brainstorming time because he knows great stories, projects and profits come from all corners of the biz.

Jeff is like you. He wants to make it happen.

Like some of you, Jeff does make it happen. A lot.

Like some others of you, Jeff knows what it's like when there's not enough happening.

He's been there.

He learned his lessons young, and if you haven't walked a mile in the Ralph Lauren moccasins of a washed-up teen star, you won't know what that's like.

Lucky for Jeff, he learned from his burns early, and by the time he was in his 20s, he could afford a Beverly Hills doctor to heal the scars. If you're facing your own career cul-de-sac and it's nowhere you'd want to point to on Blockshopper, Jeff wants to share information that might provide a roadmap out. And up.

So maybe Jeff Cohen is a little of all of the professions I mentioned at the beginning of this, and just one more: coach. And certainly a positive, engaged and uplifting one.

Entertainment is a complex, often frustrating but always challenging industry.

It's challenging to gross a billion dollars, and it's challenging to pay the rent.

It's hell on fragile egos, and it's depleted more trust funds than Charles Schwab's seen in his dreams.

It's a challenge to navigate, yet some who are sharp-witted and strong-willed not only manage to do just that but they also manage another neat trick: they endure. If we still had a Greyhound Bus Terminal on the West Side, that's where I'd send the faint of heart and soft of tush.

If you want to compete, at any level, whether it's down in the streets or up in the suites, you've got to train your brain and steel your nerves for the long-distance course.

The Dealmaker's Ten Commandments puts you in the locker room with a pretty damn good coach: Jeff Cohen.

Steven Gaydos
Vice President, Executive Editor
VARIETY

CONTENTS

WARNING

"Great and good are seldom the same man."

—Thomas Fuller

This book is about being great. This book is not about being good. They are two distinct ideas. If you want to be good, there are other books for that.

This book is a tool kit. It's a weapons cache to help you fight your way through brutal economic warfare, emerge victorious and claim your piece of the pie. It is not my aim to show you what a nice guy I am or how much I love puppies. It is my aim to provide you with real-world tactics, strategies and guiding principles to help you achieve your professional and economic goals. It's dark business created in the white hot crucible of ceaseless transactional combat.

Fire can keep you warm or it can burn down your house. Likewise, *The Dealmaker's Ten Commandments* can help you create a terrific professional life or a horrific personal life. The principles in this book have been developed for dealing with enemies, competitors, bosses and subordinates. They are wholly inappropriate for dealing with lovers, friends, family and puppies for that matter.

You have been warned.

THE DEALMAKER'S METHODOLOGY

"Man is an animal that makes bargains: no other animal does this—no dog exchanges bones with another."

—ADAM SMITH

We are all dealmakers. It's in our DNA. It's part and parcel of being a human being. Ducks swim, tigers pounce, people barter. No wonder our professional lives are overflowing with transactions. We make deals with superiors, with subordinates, with customers, with suppliers, with collaborators and competitors.

The Dealmaker's Ten Commandments provides a practical, no-nonsense methodology for negotiating deals, managing your time and handling crisis all at the highest level. This book consists of ten commandments, ten questions for self-mastery, ten tips and a healthy sprinkling of quotations.

THE DEALMAKER'S COMMANDMENTS

"The Ten Commandments were not a suggestion."

—Pat Riley

The Dealmaker's Commandments are the intellectual foundation upon which deals are made and business is conducted. Within them exists nuances and stratagems, but the commandments are the laws of physics that govern how everything interacts. Disregard them at your peril.

QUESTIONS FOR SELF-MASTERY

"It is a sad fate for a man to die too well known to everybody else, and still unknown to himself."

—Sir Francis Bacon

In law school, professors terrify their pupils by utilizing the Socratic method. Instead of answering questions, they randomly call on students and ask them questions about various court cases. It's not only effective but also quite entertaining. Watching your classmates squirm is hilarious. Getting called on and being the one squirming is less hilarious. Regardless of the entertainment quotient, Socrates instructed Plato who instructed Aristotle who instructed Alexander the Great, so it's hard to argue with the results.

Socrates believed that *"[t]he unexamined life is not worth living."* The big idea being that self-knowledge obtained by thoughtfully answering questions is the path to true wisdom. Through rigorous self-examination, we exercise the muscles of critical thinking and introspection instead of robotically regurgitating facts and figures. It is not easy, nor is it supposed to be. A number of philosophers have argued that truly knowing yourself is the most difficult thing a human being can do. I strongly suggest that you take the time to look within, contemplate and answer the ten Questions for Self-Mastery posed throughout the book. The objective is to transcend the mere acquisition of knowledge and gain wisdom. Phones can be smart; only people can be wise.

TIPS

If you don't know what tips are, you should buy a different book.

QUOTATIONS

"The wisdom of the wise and the experience of ages, may be preserved by quotation."

—Isaac D'Israeli

Quotes, quotes, quotes! Perhaps I love quotes so much because I both hunger for the "wisdom of the wise" and have a really short attention span. Speaking of quotes, here's one from Pablo Picasso: *"Good artists copy, great artists steal."* In constructing the Dealmaker's Commandments, I have stolen ideas from some of the best: Nietzsche, Lincoln, Bonaparte, Shelley and many others. The philosophy expounded in this book is an amalgam of the knowledge I have snatched from a diverse collection of intellects combined with my real-world experiences as a dealmaker. Quotation is no substitute for critical thinking and introspection, but why not use the "experience of ages" to speed us along the way?

THE END GAME

> *"Excellence is an art won by training and habituation. . . . We are what we repeatedly do. Excellence, then is not an act but a habit."*
>
> **—Aristotle**

It is my goal to help you achieve excellence as a dealmaker and perhaps learn something about yourself in the process. The Dealmaker's Ten Commandments are not a quick fix. I don't know of a button to press to instantly achieve mastery of anything. Excellence is achieved from consistent incremental improvement: baby steps, progress, forward momentum. Get in the habit of incorporating the Dealmaker's Commandments into your decision-making process. With sufficient time and habituation, it will become second nature. Opportunities that once were hidden become visible. Traps that would have snared you are avoided. Enemy vulnerabilities that would have gone undetected reveal themselves.

I'm sure you want to jump right in, but please allow me a few pages to share how the Dealmaker's Commandment came into being. My motivations are purely selfish. I'd just like to get it off my chest. Oddly enough, the genesis involves a chance encounter between a broken former child actor and a ruthless political philosopher.

CHUNK MEETS MACHIAVELLI

 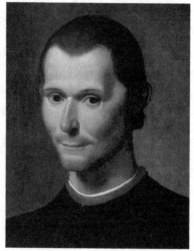

"When I was 14, I was the oldest I ever was. I've been getting younger ever since."

—Shirley Temple

There's a famous old Hollywood story about a dreadful meeting between Shirley Temple and her mega-agent, Lew R. Wasserman, the mogul of MCA. According to her biography, he told the pubescent Shirley Temple that she was "washed up." After all those hits, all the money she had made him, she had come to the end of her usefulness. The greatest child star of all time was unceremoniously fired as a client. She began to cry. Lew pushed a box of tissues her way. "Have one on me," said the great mogul.

For me, 15 was the oldest I ever was. After having some success as a child actor, my career was kaput. As a little boy, I was a cute, chubby kid and did a fair amount of work in the biz. My most notable role was playing "Chunk" in the Richard Donner/Steven Spielberg film *The Goonies* in 1985. Top of the world at age 11!

My old man was, for the most part, gone from my life by the time I was seven. My mother, little sister and I struggled financially. Things were always tense at my home growing up in the San Fernando Valley. To escape, I would watch the old 1930s *Little Rascals* shorts shown on KTLA's *Family Film Festival* hosted by local celebrity Tom Hatten. I miss that guy; he was awesome. Thanks to Tom's TV show, I knew what I wanted to do with my life. I wanted to be "Spanky," the pudgy and hilarious member of *The Little Rascals* aka "Our Gang." I was sad, but watching Spanky's antics made me happy. I wanted to make the sad people around me happy as well.

With the help of Mama Cohen, a dedicated stage mother right up there with the best of 'em, I started going on auditions. Shockingly, I actually got parts. First an air conditioner commercial, then guest spots on *Webster*, *Facts of Life*, *Family Ties* and every other 80s sitcom. (I once had to sing Prince's "Baby I'm a Star" on an episode of *Kid's Incorporated*, but I prefer to forget that one. . . .) The coup de grace? Get cast in a major motion picture directed by Richard Donner and produced by Steven Spielberg. And, I'm the funny fat kid! Move over Spanky, here comes Jeff B. Cohen! So, this is how it works. Life is pretty sweet. Now we have some dough, and my family is happy. Wow!

But just when things we're starting to hum, I faced a child actor's greatest nemesis . . . puberty.

"Chunk" was growing into a young man and losing some of his chunkiness. Those formally cute chubby cheeks now had acne on them. Auditioning for parts became awkward and nerve wracking. I even began to develop a stutter. I couldn't get jobs. I couldn't get paid. Things were a mess. Some child stars transcend adolescence and go on to have great careers in front of the camera as adults. I did not.

> *"The magic of first love is our ignorance that it can ever end."*
> **—Benjamin Disraeli**

Acting was my first love, and I was completely blindsided when it abruptly ended. Everyone liked me. I could contribute. I was good at something. I added value. I had worth. But, after puberty, there were no parts for me. I played by the rules. I sacrificed my personal dignity to get laughs. I enthusiastically gave up my childhood to go on auditions and build a career. Now it was over. A has-been before I got my learner's permit.

Looking back, it seems kind of silly, but at the time, it felt quite serious. The love of the audience had been lost and so was I.

"Depression is anger turned inward."

—**Sigmund Freud**

The system had failed me. More accurately, I had failed the system. I got mad. "Screw Hollywood!" "To hell with these casting agents!" "I am not worthless!" "I still have talent!" My actor's attempt at pleasing everyone had failed me. My modus operandi of "give to the audience and they give back" no longer worked. I was angry at the world. With no outlet, the anger turned inward. I became depressed.

That's when I met Machiavelli . . .

"Everyone sees what you appear to be, few experience what you really are."

—**Niccolò Machiavelli**

I was attending Taft High School in Woodland Hills, part of the Los Angeles Unified School District. Go Toreadors! What is a Toreador? We never quite figured that one out. Well, I had the good fortune of being in an honors program that allowed me as a high school student to take an actual bonafide college class at UCLA with real college students. Exciting! What class to take? So many options. I wanted to study something different from acting that I could be good at. How about political science? Ex-actors do really well in politics in California. Ronald Reagan, the Governator, etc. . . . Intro to Poli Sci it is.

One of the first books we read was a slim 120-pager called *The Prince* written by Niccolò Machiavelli during the politically volatile early Italian Renaissance. It's sort of a "how-to" book for a prince. How to run your state effectively. How to deal with subjects and competing monarchs. How to wage war, gain power. How to keep that power. Unlike Aristotle and Plato before him, Machiavelli didn't believe in creating an idealistic utopia. He is the father of political realism. His experience in Italian politics had led him to the conclusion that

"in general of men, that they are ungrateful, fickle, false, cowardly, covetous and as long as you succeed they are yours entirely . . ."

—**Niccolò Machiavelli**

It was the first thing I had read that made any damn sense in as long as I could remember. People are selfish and shortsighted. They will do what is in there perceived best self-interest with little regard to the consequences of those around them unless those consequences could boomerang and endanger themselves.

I was taught that to not sacrifice yourself for others was an aberration and shameful. I had given everything I had. But my need for adoration was unrequited. As William Butler Yeats wrote, *"Too long a sacrifice/Can make a stone of the heart."* I was freezing up on the inside.

Machiavelli turned my world on its head. He gave me perspective. Casting directors didn't refuse to hire me because they're bad people. They're just people. It would be utterly insane and not in their best interest to hire me if I didn't look right for the part, no matter how sweet a kid I was.

Audiences were bored of me. It's not because they're bad people. They're just people. I didn't look cute anymore, and I didn't have anything interesting to say. They should be bored of me.

Self-centered behavior is not a moral failing but a fundamental and reasonable part of human nature. It was cold but liberating. Things felt less shameful and more clinical. A real explanation for what I was observing all around me.

Machiavelli was looking for work when he wrote *The Prince*. I could empathize. His book was sort of a job application to become an advisor to the new Florentine prince, Piero di Lorenzo de' Medici, to whom he dedicated the book. "Hey, Lorenzo, if you hire me, here is some of the awesome advice I will give you."

He didn't get the job, but he did get his book banned by the Catholic Church. They registered it to the Index Librorum Prohibitorum. The Pope wasn't big on Machiavelli's political realism, I suppose. Big Mac's ideas were not politically correct for his times, but neither were Socrates', Galileo's nor Darwin's.

Reading *The Prince* made me feel like a prince. I'm just a high school kid, but I've stumbled on to this "college" book of ancient banned wisdom. What an amazing gift! How to be a prince. How to win power. How to observe humanity with perspective, in a scientific manner, where outcomes of human behavior are predictable. Nothing human is ever completely predictable, of course, but somewhat predictable, manageable. This could help me regain my bearings as a person, regain some semblance of control over my life. His insights enabled me to begin to craft a plan for adulthood. Machiavelli taught me that even though the world is tumultuous and people are myopically self-interested, great things could still be achieved if you based your decisions on how things are, not how you would like them to be. Analysis and actions need to be based upon unfettered truth not cockeyed optimism.

He advocated the virtue of adaptability. Machiavelli understood the dichotomy that although certain aspects of human behavior are eternal, the facts on the ground change constantly. He phrased it more eloquently:

"A man who is used to acting in one way never changes, he must come to ruin when the times, in changing, no longer are in harmony with his ways."

—Niccolò Machiavelli

He gave me hope that there was a way out. Feeling isolated and disappointed was not weird; it was part of the human condition. I knew that I had a gift. I could still be good at something, even though people didn't see it anymore. But, now I wasn't alone. There was a whole universe of great thinkers out there I could learn from. Machiavelli opened the door to Nietzsche and Mencken and Hobbes. I altered my perception of my position.

"There is the greatest practical benefit in making a few failures early in life."

—Thomas Henry Huxley

I began to see my experience as a child actor as a great blessing. How lucky to have experienced the cycle of success and failure at such a young age. I was young and had time to figure it out, build a second act. I was very fortunate to be accepted into UC Berkeley for my undergraduate, eventually becoming the president of the student body. **"Chunk for President!"** turned out to be an effective slogan. I guess being a former child actor had some perks after all.

I returned to UCLA for law school, and with the help of my director from *The Goonies*, the great Richard Donner, I got a job at Universal Studios in the television department to bring real-world experience to my studies. More upside to this failed actor thing . . .

"Art is the proper task of life."

—Friedrich Nietzsche

I still loved art and entertainment. I still appreciated how Spanky made me laugh and helped me escape when I was a kid. Art is eternal. It's what civilizations gift to future generations to enjoy and inspire. I wanted to find a way to add value to the entertainment industry. I discovered the moguls. I read about David Geffen in *The Operator;* Bernie Brillstein in *You're No One in Hollywood Till Someone Wants You Dead: Where Did I Go*

Right?; Louis B. Mayer in *Hollywood Raja;* Jeffrey Katzenberg in *Keys to the Kingdom;* and even our old pal Lew R. Wasserman in *The Last Mogul.*

All of these Hollywood luminaries had something in common. They were great dealmakers, each of them remarkably savvy in transactional combat. In show business (and all business for that matter), the written contract is where the rubber hits the road. All the schmoozy B.S. ends there. Read the contract, and you are faced with cold, hard economic truth. And truth was something I wanted desperately.

Yes, that's it. I'll be a dealmaker, a damn fine one.

In 2002, I co-founded a transactional media and entertainment law firm with a colleague of mine from Universal. Let's get "ready to rumble," Hollywood!

It's been a great ride so far. Over the past dozen or so years I have developed commandments, tips and tactics that guide me as a dealmaker. They have served me and my clients well. I feel very fortunate to have been rewarded economically and to have been lauded by my peers for doing something I am passionate about. Best of all, I get to help creative people create. That feels fantastic.

> *"If success is not on your own terms—if it looks good to the world but does not feel good in your own heart—it is no success at all."*
> **—Anna Quindlin**

Success is life on your own terms. The Dealmaker's Ten Commandments have helped me successfully negotiate the terms of my life, and I sincerely hope they help you successfully negotiate the terms of yours.

Now, to the maw . . .

IT IS BETTER TO BE FEARED THAN LOVED

"Love is preserved by the link of obligation which . . . is broken at every opportunity for advantage; but fear preserves you by a dread of punishment which never fails."

—NICCOLÒ MACHIAVELLI

CHAPTER OUTLINE

Why Fear Wins

We Are Wired for Fear

What's Good for the Goose

Dealmakers and Despots

Control

WHY FEAR WINS

"Since love and fear can hardly exist together, if we must choose between them, it is far safer to be feared than loved."

—Niccolò Machiavelli

Way back in the beginning of the sixteenth century, my pal from the early Italian Renaissance, Niccolò Machiavelli, analyzed the relationship between love, fear, control and power. The actual chapter in his book *The Prince* is titled "Concerning Cruelty and Clemency, and Whether It Is Better to Be Loved Than Feared." What a great title! So imposing. Makes me imagine the intrigue, romance and danger of that time in Italy. A tumultuous time indeed: warring principalities, assassinations, corruption, fratricide, patricide. You name it, they did it. And from that great period of great peril emerges remarkable works of art such as Michelangelo's *David*, da Vinci's *Mona Lisa*, Botticelli's *Birth of Venus* and Machiavelli's *The Prince*.[1]

Machiavelli was very much a part of the drama of his time. He is not writing merely from an academic perspective. He was a government official in Florentine. He witnessed the brutal methods of Cesare Borgia and his father, Pope Alexander VI, up close and personal. His advice comes from a place of real-world experience. It's for rulers in a period of ceaseless instability and peril. If the Prince gets it wrong, he doesn't just lose his job; he quite possibly loses his head. Machiavelli's cold, hard assessment of human nature is that people are fickle, self-interested and shortsighted. They behave in the manner that is in their perceived best self-interest at any given moment. A Prince's subjects will claim their undying loyalty and willingness to sacrifice *"blood, property, life and children . . . when the need is far distant."* But what happens when the Prince needs them to make sacrifices now? *"That prince who, relying entirely on their promises, has neglected other precautions, is ruined . . ."*

A Prince needs his subjects to behave in a manner that he controls. Love is an insufficient and untrustworthy mechanism. If you build your empire on love, you build your empire on mud. It is unreasonable to expect other people to put your needs above their own because they have affection for you. Conversely, it is eminently reasonable for other people to put their needs above yours. There are exceptions, of course, like a

---

1. Orson Welles' character Harry Lime has a great speech making this point in *The Third Man* (1949).

3

parent's personal sacrifices for their child. But that exception proves the rule. A parent views their child as an extension of themselves.

It is the nature of love to come and go. A rose lasts while it lasts. Now fear, on the other hand, that mechanism works quite consistently. Fear is created by a dread of punishment for running afoul of the prince. Punishment creates a consistent consequence for bad behavior. Your subjects know that the punishment for not following the rules laid down in your princely decrees is imprisonment. If they don't follow your orders, they will be swiftly incarcerated or perhaps worse. Like magic, it is now in their own best interest to follow your orders. Do you do what your boss says because you love them or because you fear being fired?

That is Machiavelli's key point. People almost always do what is in their best interest. If they know that crossing you will result in meaningful punishment, then it is in their best interest to stay on your good side.

The lion isn't the king of the jungle because the zebras love petting him.

WE ARE WIRED FOR FEAR

> *"But Jesus, when you don't have any money, the problem is food. Then you have money, it's sex. When you have both, it's health, you worry about getting rupture or something. If everything is simply jake then you're frightened of death."*
>
> **—J. P. Donleavy**

The human proclivity toward fear is not a mental frailty; it's a biological certainty. It's how our brains are wired. Evolutionarily, an organism incapable of running away from scary stuff will become extinct. If a caveman runs across a berry bush, he's feeling pretty good. Some delicious berries, the sugar provides a pleasant rush of dopamine. Then, behind the berry bush, out jumps a snarling saber-toothed tiger staring him dead in the eyes. Biology kicks in. Big time. The brain's limbic system reacts instantaneously to the threat. Adrenaline floods the body. Heartbeat increases. Breathing becomes heavy. Pupils dilate. Blood vessels constrict allowing increased blood flow to the muscles. Fight or flight? If I was advising the caveman, I would vote for flight. One on one with a saber-toothed tiger probably turns out poorly.[2]

---

2. Please see *Your Caveman Brain: Running from Predators at Work* by Manie Bosman published electronically 4/6/13 for a more in depth explanation.

That caveman lives inside of us today. Think of the nice buzz of joy when you smooch your spouse or hug your toddler. Now, think of how you would feel if you were unexpectedly downsized. You read the letter left on your desk firing you. Adrenaline starts pumping. Breathing becomes heavy. Mind is racing. How can I afford my mortgage? Where can I find another job? What about the kid's college? What the hell am I going to do? Fight or flight? Add sufficient fear, and the caveman returns.

An illuminative analysis of this phenomenon occurs in the *Review of General Psychology* article "Bad Is Stronger Than Good":

> The greater power of bad events over good ones is found in everyday events, major life events (e.g. trauma), close relationship outcomes, social network patterns, interpersonal interactions and learning processes. Bad emotions, bad parents and bad feedback have more impact than good ones, and bad information is processed more thoroughly than good. . . . From our perspective, it is evolutionarily adaptive for bad to be stronger than good. We believe that throughout our evolutionary history, organisms that were better attuned to bad things would have been more likely to survive threats and, consequently, would have increased probability of passing along their genes.[3]

Fear works because that's how we are wired.

WHAT'S GOOD FOR THE GOOSE

"An endeavor to please elders is at the bottom of high marks and mediocre careers."

—John Jay Chapman

When I was in grade school, the two scariest words in the English language were "Principal's List." If you got caught committing a crime of sufficient heinousness, a fourth grade felony of some sort, then you would have to march up to the principal's office and sign the dreaded Principal's List. We didn't know the precise ramifications, but we knew it was bad. Your name was etched in stone in some sort of permanent blacklist that followed you around for the rest of your life: the mark of Cain. If your

---

3. "Bad Is Stronger Than Good," *Review of General Psychology* 5(4), 2001: 323–370.

name was in that book, you might as well move to the rainforest and live with the mountain gorillas. They don't know about the Principal's List. So maybe you still have a shot at becoming the alpha gorilla and making something of yourself.

Fear is the key mechanism of enforcement for just about every substantive institution in our lives. You break the government's law, you go to jail. Mouth off to your boss (or heaven forbid, your boss' boss), you get fired. Don't pay your mortgage, the bank seizes your house. Get nabbed flushing cherry bombs down the toilet in the girl's bathroom, you sign the Principal's List.

The idea of preferring to be feared instead of loved is counterintuitive to just about everything we are taught. Be teacher's pet and be rewarded with good grades. Go to a good school. Get a good job. Stay on your boss' good side and get that promotion.

Sit down. Shut up. Speak when spoken to. Follow the rules. Raise your hand before you ask a question. Do your homework. Say please and thank you. Respect your elders. Listen to your mother. Play nice. Follow orders.

And if you don't? Punishment, your permanent record forever sullied, you fail.

When you are subject to the authority of the institution, usually the main mechanism for achieving success is being loved. And in the old days of spending an entire career with one employer, being loved could very well be sufficient to make it through. I imagine in some situations it still does today. The problem is, that in order to gain love you act in the institution's best interest. However, the institution also acts in the institution's best interest. You worked for the company for 20 years, gave it your all but you just became too expensive. The company needs to cut costs. They feel a 25 year-old can do your job at 75 percent proficiency and 33 percent of the cost. Adios! Enjoy the gold watch and thanks for playing.

The key to being an effective dealmaker is to be able to flip the script. To quote one of my favorite philosophers, Yoda: *"You must unlearn what you have learned."* You have to internalize the mentality of the institution. To spot opportunities for you or your client to become the bank instead of the teller, the house instead of the gambler, the team owner instead of the player. To be the punishment-wielding institution instead of being subject to the punishment-wielding institution. You determine whose name gets on the Principal's List.

The government uses fear, academic institutions use fear, corporations use fear. Hell of a coincidence, right? Perhaps, fear should become a part of your arsenal as well.

DEALMAKERS AND DESPOTS

"He's a businessman. I'll make him an offer he can't refuse."
—Mario Puzo, *The Godfather*

You may be asking, how is Machiavelli's 500-year-old advice to a prince relevant to becoming a great dealmaker today? Two reasons. First of all, human nature is eternal. For good or ill, reading Machiavelli's take on mankind rings as true today as it did in the sixteenth century. Technology has changed a great deal over the past five centuries, but the hairless apes operating the machinery have not. Second, dealmakers of all stripes are the princes of our modern capitalist system. A prince uses troops to conquer foreign lands. Dealmakers use leverage, assets and intellect to conquer new economic territories. Princes have subjects. Dealmakers have subordinates. Princes form alliances. Dealmakers form joint ventures. A prince may serve a king. A dealmaker may serve a client or corporate board.

Rodrigo Borgia gained wealth and power by negotiating for the support of the College of Cardinals to ensure his election as Pope Alexander VI. Bill Gates gained wealth and power by making sure his deal with IBM for PC-DOS was structured as a license instead of an outright sale. IBM was required to pay Gates each time they sold a computer using the software. To top it off, Gates could also license the underlying code to IBM's PC clone competitors.

Genghis Kahn was able to unite the warring nomadic tribes of Northeast Asia, expand his empire and eventually control the enormous trade wealth generated from the Silk Road. Disney was able to absorb strategic competitors Pixar, Marvel and Lucasfilm to become the largest motion picture studio in the history of entertainment.

Octavius Augustus Caesar created a triumvirate with Mark Anthony and Marcus Lepidus to defeat the assassins of Julius Caesar. Jeffrey Katzenberg created a triumvirate with Steven Spielberg and David Geffen to form SKG (aka Dreamworks) after Katzenberg was passed over by Michael Eisner to become Disney's studio head.

The key difference between the deals of Caesars and CEOs is that ancient deals were often oral in nature and enforced by the status of the person giving their word. When the emperor, prince or village Godfather makes you an offer, it's likely to be one you cannot refuse. Unless you are equally powerful, there is not going to be much negotiation. The enforceability of the agreement is based upon the Godfather's willingness to stick to the bargain. His word is his bond. . . . or perhaps not, depending on if it's in his best interest to keep the bargain. What recourse does the smaller party have? None.

In a modern society, oral agreements, as MGM Mogul Sam Goldwyn famously said, *"are not worth the paper they are printed on."* Any deal of significance is made by a written contract enforceable not by the will of the stronger party but subject to the civil courts of the land. Much like a traditional society, the odds are always stacked against the weaker party, but at least there is a system of laws in place to help ensure that the contract is enforced. In today's world, the deal, ferociously negotiated, is the key mechanism to obtain wealth and power. This is why in the age of written contracts, dealmakers are so important. You control the deal, you control the world.

CONTROL

> *"Of being feared or loved I come to the conclusion that men loving according to their own will and fearing according to that of the prince, a wise prince should establish himself on that which is in his control and not the control of others."*
>
> **—Niccolò Machiavelli**

A prince, a capitalist, a dealmaker needs to be in control of their destiny and mold the world to their vision. Wielding fear at your election grants you control over the behavior of others. Attempting to win someone's love at their election does not grant you control over the behavior of others. Thus, it is better to be feared than loved.

TIP

BEWARE THE CHAIR
The King Is Dead. Long Live the King!

Thrones are imposing pieces of furniture. To start with, they usually have really intricate craftsmanship. Some are adorned with gold paint that has real gold in it. Most seem to have really nice upholstery. The one from *Game of Thrones* is made of bones and swords. That'll make you think twice about mouthing off to the king.

Thrones aren't just for monarchs. Executives have them as well. Instead of calling their thrones "thrones," it's more elegant to call it "the chair." The chair sits behind a nice desk in a nice office. Perhaps it's the office of the president of a film studio or the executive vice-president of a big talent agency or the senior viceroy viscount of development at a television production company. The plebeians humbly approach the chair with various requests. Please make my movie. Please be my talent agent. Please buy my television pitch. The chair grants its occupant power. Sometimes a great deal of power.

Having a chair can be quite intoxicating, but who makes good decisions when they're intoxicated? After a time, executives begin to believe that the power they wield emanates from themselves instead of from the chair. Then, something unexpected happens to separate the executives from their chair: corporate downsizing, a regime change or perhaps retribution for green-lighting a couple of box-office bombs? Regardless, the executive has lost their chair. The plebeians that once approached the executive now humbly approach the new occupant of the chair with their requests. The Studio President is dead. Long live the Studio President!

There is nothing wrong with sitting in a prominent chair or desiring to. Play it right, and there is tons of dough to be made. But, don't forget that your power comes from that chair. Do you have a plan if your chair is unceremoniously repossessed? If you do, great! If you do not, beware the chair. In Hollywood, without power, things can get very chilly very fast.

QUESTION FOR SELF-MASTERY

SO WHAT?

"There are more things, Lucilius, that frighten us than injure us, and we suffer more in imagination than in reality."

—Seneca

What are you afraid of? What keeps you up at night? Money fears? Health fears? Relationship fears? Afraid you're going to be a failure just like your old man? Afraid she'll never love you if she knows the truth? Afraid you're going to die alone?

Take 15 minutes. Get real, get dark. Ask yourself, "What am I most afraid of?" Write down your answers. (Note: Be sure to destroy the evidence after the exercise. This info is for your eyes only, and you should feel completely unfettered from the judgment of others. I'm not paranoid; I'm prepared.)

Your enemies are going to attempt to use your fears to their advantage, so it's best to head them off at the pass. Knowing your fears and controlling them empowers you and disempowers the opposition. You can't think straight when you're scared.

How to control our fears? I've found a marvelously effective technique used by Andy Warhol.

I know that sounds odd, but hang with me. Warhol grew up as an extremely sickly child in a working-class neighborhood in Pittsburg. He was often bedridden and developed skin pigmentation blotchiness as a complication from scarlet fever. He became a hypochondriac. As a young man he was extremely self-conscious of his appearance and was isolated because of his awkward manner and sexual orientation. He was afraid. Afraid of being rejected by his crushes. Afraid of his art being rejected by his contemporaries. Eventually, Warhol devised a truly elegant solution to manage these debilitating fears:

> *"Sometimes people let the same problem make them miserable for years when they could just say, 'so what?' That's one of my favorite things to say. 'So what?' . . . I don't know how I made it through all the years before I learned how to do that trick. It took me a long time for me to learn it, but once you do, you never forget."*
>
> **—Andy Warhol**

Take another 15 minutes and go through your list of fears one by one. Ask yourself, if this happened, "So what?" Would you still survive? Would you be put in jail for life? Would you starve to death? Would you never find anyone who would want to go to the movies with you?

Of course, we must be responsible for our fate and take all appropriate actions to prevent bad things from happening. But, it is counterproductive and a tremendous waste of energy to be a slave to the fear that those bad things *might* occur. They don't pay you to worry. Next time you're afraid that something bad might happen or if something troubling actually does happen, ask yourself "So what?" You may find that asking that little question defangs your fears, disables your foes and helps you get some sleep at night.

OUR JOURNEY THUS FAR . . .

DEALMAKER'S COMMANDMENT I: IT IS BETTER TO BE FEARED THAN LOVED.

Being feared is more useful and reliable than being loved.

Now, to discern what drives the deal.

DEALMAKER'S COMMANDMENT II: POWER LEADS; REASON FOLLOWS.

Lead, follow or be trampled asunder.

POWER LEADS;
REASON FOLLOWS

"All things are subject to interpretation. Whichever interpretation prevails

at a given time is a function of power and not truth."

—FRIEDRICH NIETZSCHE

CHAPTER OUTLINE

The Narrative of Power

The Power Punishment
Paradigm

Appetites and Aversions:
Punishment's Myriad Forms

Reason Triumphs in the
Long Run

THE NARRATIVE OF POWER

"rationalize: to bring in accord with reason or cause something to seem reasonable"

—Webster's Dictionary

In the Wild West of the 1860s, Mark Twain was working for a newspaper while living in the silver-mining boom town of Virginia City, Nevada. Legend has it one evening he was confronted by an armed robber who pulled out his revolver. *"Hand over your money!"* Mark Twain looked down at the pistol, looked up at the gunman and said: *"You sir, pose a powerful argument."*

That anecdote illustrates the power dynamic of the dealmaking process in a nutshell. The more powerful party holds a gun to the head of the weaker party and takes their money. A loaded sidearm with the hammer cocked back poses a powerful argument indeed. Of course, in practice, the process is rarely that cut and dry, but you get the idea. The party that most effectively wields power determines the outcome of the transaction.

POWER LEADS

During the dealmaking process, a "Narrative of Power" is created to justify the outcome, to rationalize the result. The more powerful party is not taking advantage of the weaker party. Of course not! The multi-billion dollar studio has a lot of overhead to cover and can only afford to pay the screenwriter the bare minimum to acquire their script. Cost-cutting measures. Got to stay lean and mean for the shareholders, right? The film cost $20 million to make and has grossed $200 million at the box office. Yes, the writer is entitled to 1 percent of the net profits, but the film has still not broken a profit. You know those foreign distribution expenses can really add up. But we're all so proud that the writer's work is resonating with audiences. Isn't that what really matters? Isn't that what we're all in it for? Sorry, our CEO couldn't join the meeting. He's flying in the studio's private jet to Sun Valley to go skiing this weekend. He sends his regards.

POWER LEADS; REASON FOLLOWS

There are always reasons to justify why the powerful party gets what they want out of a deal and why the weaker party does not. But, have no doubt, power is the mighty freight train barreling down the track. Reason is the little, red caboose tagging along for the ride.

This begs the question, why even create The Narrative of Power? What's the point?

- **Further Disempower the Weaker Party:** The smaller party may actually have power that they don't realize. If they feel they are being taken advantage of by the larger party, they might put up a more robust fight and get better terms out of the transaction. The Narrative of Power compels the losing party to subvert their disappointment by rationalizing the end result. Yes, the final terms of the deal stink. But, that's what I deserve!

- **Allow the Stronger Party to Seize the Moral High Ground:** Sometimes taking the money is just not enough. Why not take the moral high ground away from the smaller party and complete the victory? The Narrative of Power allows the larger party to justify why it is right and good and fair for the transaction to come out so strongly in their favor. Maintaining this moral high ground is a chip to be used later. Perhaps, it is used for PR purposes. To present a good face to the industry. Perhaps, it is used as leverage against the smaller party to weaken their resolve on subsequent negotiations. "You owe us; we were there for you in the beginning." Or maybe, just use that chip to rationalize away any pesky misgivings about being a greedy pig. What fun is it to be rich if you hate yourself? Just because a film makes ten times its budget doesn't mean its profit participants should be paid out, right? Oh, waiter! Another dry martini, please.

Whether we are the more powerful party or the weaker party, we are all human beings. As human beings we crave order, stability and fairness. That's why movies have happy endings. It is psychologically disconcerting to be a part of a dealmaking process where raw power overrides reason. The Narrative of Power is rationalization. This comports with a clinical definition of rationalization as:

> a defense mechanism in which controversial behaviors or feelings are justified and explained in a seemingly rational or logical manner to avoid the true explanation, and are made consciously tolerable—or ever admirable and superior—by plausible means.[1]

Please keep in mind that I am not arguing **Dealmaker's Commandment II: Power Leads; Reason Follows** is right or wrong, good or

---

1. Please see en.wikipedia.org/wiki/Rationalization (sociology) for further discussion.

bad. I'm in no position to moralize. Sometimes, I represent David. Sometimes I represent Goliath. I'm just saying that this is how deals are actually made. The party that most effectively wields power drives the outcome of the transaction. Then, a Narrative of Power is created to rationalize the final outcome. As a dealmaker, it is crucial to understand this process and recognize that the Narrative of Power is likely a convenient fiction. Don't drink the Kool-Aid and accept it as gospel. To do so is drunk dealmaking. It impairs your judgment.

THE POWER PUNISHMENT PARADIGM: PUNISHMENT → FEAR → CONTROL → POWER

"Men are not hanged for stealing horses but that horses may not be stolen."

—George Savile

In a negotiation, the dominant side will exert their power to obtain favorable terms and then create a Narrative of Power to smooth things over. But how does one obtain that power in the first place? Where does it come from?

In its rawest form, power is derived from punishment. The ability to punish behavior detrimental to your interests is the key source of a dealmaker's power. Punishing your enemies makes them fear you. If they fear you, you can control them. If you can control them, you have power. Power leads. Wielding power enables your interests to dominate the negotiation. Thus, by combining **Dealmaker's Commandment I: It Is Better to Be Feared Than Loved** with **Dealmaker's Commandment II: Power Leads; Reason Follows,** we arrive at the **Power Punishment Paradigm**:

Punishment → Fear → Control → Power

Please forgive my alliteration, it helps me remember stuff. The Power Punishment Paradigm is indispensable because bad behavior requires consequences. Let me repeat, bad behavior requires consequences. One more time, let's say it together, with feeling, **"BAD BEHAVIOR REQUIRES CONSEQUENCES."**

Some examples of bad behavior? Compensating you or your client below a fair market rate, overtly lying to you, going around your back to try to pressure your client directly, not adhering to contractual obligations, getting clever in how profit participations are calculated, threatening you or your client, impugning your reputation in the marketplace, to name a few.

This may sound coarse, but you must train the opposing side of the transaction like an animal. If your opposition acts in a manner contrary to your interests, they are punished, every time. Consistency is key. Like training your dog not to pee on the carpet. This consistent cause and effect of bad behavior creating discomfort through punishment leads to fear. The opposing side is learning that if they act against your interests there is an uncomfortable consequence en route. There is a cost to screwing with you.

The dealmaker is now feared. By utilizing this dread of punishment, the dealmaker is able to control the opposing party's actions. The deal is going to look the way I want it to look. The opposing side begins to come around and agree to the terms you want, because if they do not, they will be punished. By being able to exert this control, the dealmaker has obtained power. Next step, bend the deal to your will. Then, be a sport, construct a Narrative of Power that makes everyone feel better about the end result. This is the arc of the Power Punishment Paradigm. Punishment begets fears which begets control which begets power.

Please keep in mind that the Power Punishment Paradigm is textbook. It is straightforward to illustrate the principles at work. In practice, it is very rare for only one party to have a complete monopoly on punishment, thus the complete monopoly on power. Like any war, in transactional combat the opposing sides have various forms and degrees of punishment that they can inflict upon each other to attempt to achieve their aims.

APPETITES AND AVERSIONS: PUNISHMENT'S MYRIAD FORMS

"Intemperance is naturally punished with diseases; rashness, with mischance; injustice, with violence of enemies; pride, with ruin; cowardice, with oppression; and rebellion with slaughter."
—**Thomas Hobbes**

How then to punish your opponent? So many choices, but to find the most effective method, let's start with the ideas of seventeenth-century political philosopher Thomas Hobbes. Good ol' Hobbes believed that people behave like little particles bouncing around the earth. We jump this way and that way being controlled by our "appetites and aversions." We are pulled toward and pursue things that we want—our appetites. We are repelled and run away from things we fear and don't want—our aversions. Hobbes rightly understood that desires and fears are not universally shared but particular to each person: *"appetites, and aversions; in different tempers, customs and doctrines of men, are different."*

All forms of punishment reverse the natural order envisioned by Hobbes. Punishment pulls people away from their appetites and pushes them toward their aversions. Analyze your opposition. What do they want? What do they fear? What are their particular appetites and aversions? Is there a strategic vulnerability? Someplace they are particularly weak? Next, look at your arsenal. What weapons to punish do you have at your disposal? You might be surprised. Let's take a look and some traditional methods to injure your opponent:

- **Termination:** If you are an employer or hiring an independent contractor you have the power to fire someone. That's straightforward and powerful. Especially if they need the gig.
- **Empower Their Competition:** They don't want to play fair? Fine. Sell your wares to their mortal enemy. As the saying goes, "The enemy of my enemy is my friend."
- **Strike:** Take your ball and go home. Turn off the lights. Even if your client has a multi-year contract in place, perhaps they don't feel like showing up for work. See if the broadcaster can make the television show without the key talent. This is especially effective if you are doing collective bargaining (i.e., representing the entire cast of a project) in a renegotiation of their existing deals. The other side may sue you, but they are not going to have a television show, which is what they really want.
- **Litigation:** Reach out and sue someone. Maybe they are in breach of contract. Maybe they've tortiously interfered with an important business relationship. Maybe you have deeper pockets and want to bleed them dry. You've been served...
- **Humiliation:** Drop some unflattering tidbits in the press. Drag their name through the mud. Corporations especially hate bad press, because their shareholders do. If you have a good relationship with a reporter or a million social media followers, this can be an extremely cost-effective tactic.
- **Block Access:** Do you have access to something your opponent wants? Do they want to join some swanky club you are a member of? Are you best pals with a person they desperately want to know?

Are you well connected in a new area of business they want to enter? Block 'em. "You may not pass!"

- **Excommunication:** I've saved the best for last. George Bernard Shaw said that *"Silence is the most perfect expression of scorn."* I very much agree. Furthermore, excommunication is the perfect expression of silence. When you excommunicate someone, you are effectively killing them. They no longer exist. They have no place in your life. They are unworthy of your time or your energy. You have decided that they have no value and made them a ghost. The nice thing about excommunication is that anyone can do it. You don't have to hire an expensive lawyer or know someone in the press or be someone's boss. You just have to make a decision and stick to it. That power resides within you. Excommunicating a mortal enemy may seem twisted, but it can also be oddly liberating and ultimately empowering. A helpful by-product is that it frees up your energy to focus on more productive and lucrative relationships.

Punishment, punishment, punishment. Dark business indeed. But, it's supposed to be dark. You're supposed to be feared not loved, right? Yes, but don't go nuts. You don't punish without reason, and you don't do it because you're a sadist. You're not a lunatic; you're a dealmaker. You do it to train your opponents. Bad behavior requires consequences. Screwing with you or your client comes with a cost. After sufficient punishment, your opponents realize this. Good, they got the message. No need for further fisticuffs. We're all capitalists. Let's make a deal.

REASON TRIUMPHS IN THE LONG RUN

"In the long run we are all dead."

—John Maynard Keynes

The good news is that in the long run reason does prevail over power. A system can't subvert the truth forever. If you're on the side of the good guys, hopefully you're still alive when the Ewoks defeat the stormtroopers on planet Endor. The problem is that a deal is not a movie. It's a still photograph. A deal is a snapshot of the parties' relative power and interests at the particular moment in time when the deal is made. If the weaker party gains enough strength and the reality of the situation evolves too far beyond the terms of the deal, it will not hold. Perhaps, a renegotiation is called for? And during that renegotiation, power will lead, and reason will follow yet again. If reason has gained sufficient traction to make it powerful then the Narrative of Power will actually coincide with the truth. This can take a while so don't hold your breath.

MANAGING POWER

"Nearly all men can stand adversity, but if you want to test a man's character, give him power."

—**Abraham Lincoln**

Honest Abe was not kidding. As difficult as it is to gain a base of power, it's just as difficult to effectively manage it. Something about having all that juice flowing through you can change a person. Power leads; reason follows. Yes, but you must be able to manage and grow your power to expand your empire as a dealmaker. Here are some thoughts on how to effectively manage it.

- **Treat Power Like Money:** Power is a finite resource and an intoxicating one at that. Invest power like money. Spend it judiciously and appropriately. If you invest your power wisely, it will grow and you will have more. Blow it on an infantile bender and good luck getting it back.
- **Recognize Its Source:** Just because you have power, doesn't mean you are the source of your power. Perhaps your power comes from representing an important director or controlling the film rights to a popular book or having a good executive position (i.e., the "chair"). It's important to remember that many times you are a vessel for someone or something else's power. Keep this in mind to prevent your head from getting too big.
- **Use It for a Defined Purpose:** Remember that power is not an end in itself. It is a tool, like a hammer or a spreadsheet or a toaster. Don't use power capriciously. Use it to obtain specific, rational, measured objectives.
- **Don't Believe the Hype:** When I was a kid, I had a small role in a production of Tennessee William's *Cat on a Hot Tin Roof* at the Los Angeles Music Center. The part of "Big Daddy" was played by the great character actor Pat Hingle. The reviews had just come out and were very favorable to Pat. I went to his dressing room and said, "Wow, did you read these reviews?" He said that he hadn't. I was totally confused and asked why? He told me that he never read his reviews because "If I believe the good things they write about me, then I'd have to believe the bad things they write about me too."

As your power grows, there will be a lot of hype and noise. It's easy to let the adulation distract you and prevent you from thinking straight. Don't let it. Forget the chatter. Mind your knitting. Focus on doing great work. Like Pat said, if you believe the good things they write about you, then you'd have to believe the bad things they write about you too.

QUESTION FOR SELF-MASTERY

WHAT IS MY PEG?

"Most people do not really want freedom, because freedom involves responsibility, and most people are frightened of responsibility."
—Sigmund Freud

They train circus elephants not to run away in this really clever and terrible manner. They chain the mighty behemoth to a metal pole that is driven 15 feet into the ground. Really deep down there. The elephant tries to run away, to pull the pole out of the ground. Tries and tries and tries, but can't do it. It's not possible, the pole is too deep. No amount of elephantine effort could dislodge that pole. Eventually, the elephant stops trying, gives up. The elephant has been trained, domesticated as it were. The mighty jungle giant no more. When the elephant goes on the road with the circus, it would be too difficult to drive a pole 15 feet into the ground. You need special machinery and such. So they plant a peg 4 feet down instead. The elephant could easily pull the peg out of the ground and make a break for it. But, they don't. They assume that the 4 foot peg is the 15 foot pole. That mean old imaginary pole still has power over them. It's sad. This mighty beast held back by a tiny peg. If they tried again, they could bail on the circus and escape to Yellowstone National Park. Maybe they could make friends with the buffalos. Live the good life!

Ask yourself, "What is my peg?" What has power over you? What's holding you back? Sometimes, it can feel oddly comfortable to be chained to something. Less freedom means less responsibility. Conversely more freedom means greater responsibility and thus greater power. That can be daunting, but perhaps it's time to give it a shot. Have you tried to free yourself lately? You are a mighty elephant, ya know? Maybe that 15 foot pole you are chained to is really just a 4 foot peg?

OUR JOURNEY THUS FAR . . .

DEALMAKER'S COMMANDMENT I: IT IS BETTER TO BE FEARED THAN LOVED.

Being feared is more useful and reliable than being loved.

DEALMAKER'S COMMANDMENT II: POWER LEADS; REASON FOLLOWS.

Power, not reason, drives the outcome of a transaction.

We know the philosophical fundamentals; now let's turn our attention toward our foes.

DEALMAKER'S COMMANDMENT III: EVERYONE IS ON THE SAME SIDE . . . THEIR OWN.

Come to think of it, let's keep an eye on our "friends" as well . . .

EVERYONE IS ON THE SAME SIDE ... THEIR OWN

"Men are moved by two levers only: fear and self-interest."

—NAPOLEON BONAPARTE

CHAPTER OUTLINE

Know the Combatants

Survey the Battlefield

The Motivation Mosaic

"Perceived" Best
Self-Interest

The Will to Power

The Motivation Mosaic's
Most Important Piece

KNOW THE COMBATANTS

"If you know the enemy and know yourself you need not fear the results of a hundred battles."

—Sun Tzu

The battle has commenced. The negotiation has begun. We are coming in hot! The time has come to analyze the combatants and discover what motivates them. No easy task, it's an art and a science.

First the basics, who is on the other side? Who is in the forefront? Who is in the shadows? Who is calling the shots? Perhaps you are negotiating against a corporation. Who is the executive on point for representing the corporation's interests? Is this person really the decision maker? Do they have the power to say no, but not the power to say yes? Who is their boss? What is their collective transactional reputation? Aggressive? Docile? Sneaky? Trustworthy? Perhaps you rep the corporation and are negotiating against an individual. Who reps them? Is it a lawyer, talent agent, talent manager, or all three? Who has the client's ear? Which rep is pulling the strings or is the talent actually hands-on in negotiating the deal?

Who are the stakeholders on your side? Are you the principal or a representative negotiating on behalf of a principal? Are there other representatives/advisors in the mix? Who is lead on your side?

Once we know the players, let's discover their motivations and the deal's sources of power. The best place to start is with the golden rule: *Whoever has the gold makes the rules.* What person or entity is the wealthiest party to the transaction? They are likely the most powerful. What are they getting out of the deal? What do they want? What Narrative of Power is being constructed to justify their desires?

What are the spoils being negotiated for? What property is changing hands? What services are being provided? Who owns the final product being created? Does the deal have a fundamental/linchpin-like quality for the acquirer or is it merely ancillary? Is it cake, or is it just the frosting?

A lot of questions. Yes, but questions that need to be answered.

SURVEY THE BATTLEFIELD

"The battlefield is a scene of constant chaos. The winner will be the one who controls that chaos, both his own and the enemies."
—**Napoleon Bonaparte**[1]

We must survey the transactional battlefield from both a macroeconomic and microeconomic perspective. Regarding the macro, what does the other side as a whole want? What is the other side as a whole afraid of? What does the other side as a whole perceive to be in its best interest? What are the appetites and aversions of the opposing side holistically?

Apply the same macroeconomic analysis to your side. What does your side as a whole want? What does your side as a whole perceive to be in its best interest? What are the appetites and aversions of your side holistically?

Now, it's time to look at the individual atoms bouncing around the deal, the microeconomic analysis. Look at each of the individual players comprising the opposing side. What motivates each one of them? How are they being paid? How are they rewarded in their particular power structure? Are they trying to show their boss how aggressive they can be to finally get that promotion? Do they have their first kid on the way and want to keep everything peaceful so they don't risk getting fired? How do the elements that comprise the other side relate to each other? Who will likely take the fall if things go south with the deal? Who will get the credit if things go well? And, of course above all, what do they fear? Apply the same microeconomic analysis to your side. Things can get quite complex, quite quickly. However, without this analysis, you are flying blind.

THE MOTIVATION MOSAIC

"Everything should be made as simple as possible, but not simpler."
—**Albert Einstein**

The macro appetites and aversions of each side combined with the micro appetites and aversions of each side create a fluid system of perceived

---

1. I apologize for all of the Napoleon quotes I use in this section. I blame him. When it comes to astute battlefield analysis, he's hard to beat.

self-interests, which I call **The Motivation Mosaic**. The Motivation Mosaic is always in flux and can change at any given point within the deal for an infinite number of reasons. Perhaps a client fires one of their representatives. Perhaps the stock market tanks. Perhaps a corporate party to the transaction gets acquired by a larger company. Perhaps the ratings of the television show you are negotiating for spike or dip.

Processing all of this information can be overwhelming, but after sufficient experience, it becomes second nature. There are reoccurring patterns within the Motivation Mosaic that occur time and time again: The self-sabotaging client who kills a deal because they are secretly afraid of failure; The well-paid cocky corporate executive who overplays their hand; The skittish rep who will make no decisions on the deal so they are clear to throw another team member under the bus in case anything goes wrong. In essence, the Motivation Mosaic is a three-dimensional map of the battlefield and the combatants in real time.

"PERCEIVED" BEST SELF-INTEREST

"Never stop your enemy when they are making a mistake."
—Napoleon Bonaparte

When formulating a deal's Motivation Mosaic, we assume that each individual involved with the transaction is pursuing their own perceived best self-interest. I use the word "perceived" because we cannot assume that just because a party believes something to be in their best self-interest, it actually is. As an experienced dealmaker, you have the benefit of working on a large number of transactions in a variety of areas. You have created countless Motivation Mosaics. You will likely recognize traps and misconceptions that have snared other parties into wanting things that actually leave them vulnerable and weaken their position. Things that they "perceive" are in their best self-interests, might actually be harmful to them. Perhaps someone is focusing all their energy on getting a profit participation instead of upfront compensation, and you know that the profit participation will never pay off. Perhaps someone is expending a tremendous amount of political capital and burning bridges to impress a client who is going to fire them after the deal is complete. Perhaps someone is so focused on making sure the minute legalese of a contract is perfect that they are not paying attention to big picture economic issues that actually matter. If those parties are on your side, feel free to let them know. If they are on the other side, make sure they have plenty of rope to hang themselves.

THE WILL TO POWER

"Physiologists should think before putting down the instinct of self preservation as the cardinal instinct of an organic being. A living thing seeks above all to discharge its strength. Life itself is will to power; self preservation is only one of the indirect and most frequent results."
—Friedrich Nietzsche

So what does each party perceive to be in their best interest? There is no easy answer, but we have a methodology to help paint the picture. How are they impacted by the macroeconomics? How are they impacted by the microeconomics? What are their appetites and aversions? Are they just trying to eke out as much dough as possible or is there more to it?

When creating the deal's Motivation Mosaic, keep in mind Nietzsche's idea of the Will to Power. Nietzsche disagreed with the commonly held notion that the universal motivation of all organisms is survival. Nietzsche wondered that if survival was the dominant instinct, why would people ever choose to put their life at risk? Why do people jump off of a bridge tied to a bungee cord or become bull fighters or race cars at 200 miles per hour? He believed that the dominant impulse in certain individuals is the desire to increase their power, even if sometimes this endangered their survival. He felt that for these people happiness was achieved not through mere survival but that *"Happiness is the feeling that power increases—that resistance is being overcome."*

Keep the Will to Power in mind when crafting your Motivation Mosaic. In addition to self-preservation, fear and economic interests, parties are influenced by their impulse to expand their domain, to take risks in order to expand their empire. The Will to Power not only influences individuals but organizations as well. Is the other side more interested in destroying your client to demonstrate their power than in making a buck? Are they willing to sacrifice their short-term economic interests in order to increase their sphere of influence in the long term?

THE MOTIVATION MOSAIC'S MOST IMPORTANT PIECE

"Modern man lives under the illusion that he knows what he wants, while he actually wants what he is supposed to want."

—**Eric Fromm**

Everyone is on the same side . . . their own. Everyone wants what they believe is best for themselves. Fine. Humans are human. It is what it is. But that still leaves the most important part of the Motivation Mosaic: You. What do you want out of this little war? What are your appetites? What are your aversions? Don't forget to add your piece to the Motivation Mosaic; that's the most important piece of all.

NEVER GIVE ANYONE AN ANGLE

"To have a good enemy, choose a friend: He knows where to strike."

—**Diane De Poitiers**

If everyone is on their own side, what conclusion does this lead to? Sadly, you can never give anyone an angle to take a clean shot at you. If you exhibit weakness to your side or the opposing side, if you share a vulnerability that can be used against you later, if you divulge a piece of information that can come back to haunt you, if you lose your cool in a situation that requires composure, if you appear unprepared at an important moment in the negotiation, you are in danger.

Pressing "reply all" instead of "reply." An inopportune tweet. A bawdy Facebook post. Getting tipsy and divulging a sensitive piece of information at the office Christmas Party. You have given up your power to someone who now has an angle, a way to damage you at their election. Your power now lies in the trigger finger of the one looking at you through that magnified scope on their sniper rifle. They have a clean shot. Maybe they pull the trigger, maybe they don't. If your interests continue to overlap and they behave in a rational economic manner, then they have no incentive to shoot, right? But what if they aren't feeling particularly rational that day? What if they perceive that your interests are no longer aligned? Are they going to pull the trigger? It's their call, not yours. Being a dealmaker is about having control of your destiny. You have lost that control and are reduced to depending on "the kindness of strangers." Let's see how that works out.

WHO IS MY BRUTUS?

"Et tu, Brute?"

—Julius Caesar

When Julius Caesar walked into the Roman Senate in 44 BC, he was probably feeling pretty good. His military victories had expanded the Roman Empire's territory as far as the English Channel and the Rhine. His immense popularity and power allowed him to be declared "Dictator in Perpetuity." A great gig, if you can get it. But, on the Ides of March, a group of dagger-wielding assassins led by his "friend" Marcus Junius Brutus, whom he had appointed to political office, put an end to that "in Perpetuity" stuff. Apparently, Caesar initially fought the attackers, but when he saw that Brutus was among them, he covered his face with his toga and resigned himself to his fate.

In 1956, the three living Warner Brothers, Jack, Harry and Albert, sold the studio they founded to a Boston banking syndicate. They had spent five decades building something great together. Time to cash out and move on. Well, time for Harry and Albert to move on anyway. What they didn't know was that their brother Jack Warner was covertly controlling the sale. After the brothers sold to the syndicate, Jack immediately bought back a majority of the shares under the table and, as the largest shareholder of Warner Brothers, immediately declared himself president of the studio. When Harry discovered the ruse by reading an article in *Variety*, he suffered a heart attack followed by a stroke and had to walk with a cane for the rest of his life. Albert and Harry never spoke to Jack Warner again.

These are two extreme examples, but you get the idea. Betrayals from within happen every day. The insider has the best opportunity to do the greatest damage. Take a hard look around your operation. Ask yourself, "Who is my Brutus?" This may seem like an exercise in paranoia, and to a degree it is. But still, ask the question. Who would most likely be the one to sharpen the dagger and drive it into your back? Are there any precautions you can take to make sure that doesn't happen? Maybe there's nothing to worry about. Maybe there is. Either way, keep your eyes open. One can never be too cautious.

OUR JOURNEY THUS FAR ...

DEALMAKER'S COMMANDMENT I: IT IS BETTER TO BE FEARED THAN LOVED.

Being feared is more useful and reliable than being loved.

DEALMAKER'S COMMANDMENT II: POWER LEADS; REASON FOLLOWS.

Power, not reason, drives the outcome of a transaction.

DEALMAKER'S COMMANDMENT III: EVERYONE IS ON THE SAME SIDE ... THEIR OWN.

Parties are motivated by and can be predicted to behave in accordance with their perceived best self-interests.

Now, to check our specs.

DEALMAKER'S COMMANDMENT IV: THINGS ARE PRECISELY AS THEY SEEM.

Is seeing believing?

DEALMAKER'S COMMANDMENT

IV

THINGS ARE PRECISELY AS THEY SEEM

"Things are entirely what they appear to be — and behind them . . . there is nothing."

—JEAN-PAUL SARTRE

CHAPTER OUTLINE

Abandon All Hope

Ockham's Razor

Eliminate Pride

Eliminate Envy

Eliminate Lust

Eliminate Anger

Eliminate Morality

Intellectual Freedom

ABANDON ALL HOPE

"Hope is a waking dream."

—Aristotle

Human beings are hopeful by nature, which is beautiful. We want to think the best of people and that everything will be coming up roses. Why else are people still paying good money to hear Little Orphan Annie belt out "The Sun Will Come out Tomorrow"? We know our kids are all going to grow up to be president. We are going to build a fortune rivaling Mark Zuckerberg's. Harvard Law School is going to love my witty personal statement (they did not love my witty personal statement btw . . .). We are going to hit our goal weight before bikini season or Speedo season, as the case may be. It's all going to work out.

And all that good-natured enthusiasm has its purpose. Perhaps it's motivation to work hard and be a good parent, spouse or employee. Perhaps it's an alluring fantasy to keep one sane. Great, it has its place.

Its place is not here.

To be a great dealmaker you have to make great choices. To make great choices you must see things as they are, not how you want them to be. This is a deceptively difficult thing to do. As human beings our emotions, desires, prejudices and fears cloud our judgment. We have stimulus upon stimulus lobbying, cajoling and bribing our intellect to make the wrong call. In addition to the internal forces impacting our judgment, there are myriad outside pressures from competitors and collaborators and clients pulling us this way and that.

We have surveyed the battlefield, now the hard part: to process the information and render the correct judgment. This is what you get paid the big bucks for.

Dealmaker's Commandment IV: Things Are Precisely as They Seem is the mechanism to shave away desire and prejudice and morality and hope in order to discover truth. And it begins with a Franciscan friar and logician from fourteenth-century England named William of Ockham.

OCKHAM'S RAZOR

"Plurality must never be posited without necessity."
—Ockham's Razor/William of Ockham

William of Ockham's great contribution to science was putting forth the idea that when you have two competing theories, you should favor the one that has the least underlying assumptions. Scientists use Ockham's Razor to scrape away unnecessary information and complexity to arrive at the simplest equation possible. It takes the idea that the shortest distance between two points is a straight line and applies it to the scientific method. The most straightforward interpretation of what you are observing is most likely the correct one. Things are precisely as they seem. Sir Isaac Newton said it more elegantly: *"We are to admit no more causes of natural things than such are both true and sufficient to explain their appearances."*

Basically, when you walk in your bedroom and find your best friend in bed with your wife and she says: *"This isn't what it looks like!"* It's precisely what it looks like.

ELIMINATE PRIDE: CONFIRMATION BIAS

"I beseech you, in the bowels of Christ, think it possible that you may be mistaken."

—Oliver Cromwell

Confirmation Bias is a common phenomenon in cognitive science and psychology where people exhibit a tendency to search for or interpret information in a way that confirms their preexisting beliefs. Confirmation bias can lead to such fantastic results as **belief perseverance** even after a position is shown to be a demonstrably false and **illusory correlation,** where people mistakenly connect two unrelated events.[1] We must strive for objectivity to counter confirmation bias. First facts, then analysis.

How then to deal with our prejudices? That's a tricky one. To some degree, prejudice is necessary to live. We prejudge that when we turn a door knob the door will open. We prejudge that when we smell a rose it will be fragrant. These are great bets. We also prejudge that a person's previous behavior is indicative of their future behavior. If the party we were negotiating against was a lying SOB on the last deal, they will be a lying SOB on this deal. If our opponent folded when litigation was threatened on the last deal, the same threat will work on this deal. These are good bets, but not great bets.

---

1. Please see en.wikipedia.org/wiki/Confirmation_bias for further discussion.

Beware of fighting the last war. Let your opponent's prior behavior inform your analysis, but do not be a slave to it. Has the company you are negotiating against increased in size and power since your last melee? Has the popularity of the writer you are negotiating for decreased since their last film bombed? Be mindful of today's battlefield conditions. Where is the risk now? Where is the reward now?

The relative power of the parties and the strategies utilized by their representatives are fluid, not static. As the legal proverb states, *"A good judge conceives quickly but judges slowly."* Let your prejudgments be the beginning of your analysis, not the end of it.

Confirmation Bias is really a form of pride. We want our initial take on a situation to be correct. It feels good to be right. Conversely, being wrong is a blow to our ego and wounds our pride. But, remember that all pride's wounds are self-inflicted.[2] Our allies need the correct answer, not the answer that makes us the smartest guy in the room. There is no shame in being mistaken. However, there is shame in not being able to change your opinion when evidence suggests you should. Be strong enough to shave away your pride and see things as they are.

ELIMINATE ENVY: PUT ON YOUR BLINDERS

"Ignore your competition. A Mafia guy in Vegas gave me this advice: 'Run your own race, put on your blinders.' Don't worry about how others are doing. Something better will come."

—Joan Rivers

There's a reason they put blinders on racehorses. To have a shot at winning, the horses must be able to run straight ahead and not be distracted by their competitors. To be a great dealmaker, one must put on a pair of envy blinders. This is no small task. In entertainment there is a daily ritual of checking key trade publications (i.e., *Variety, The Hollywood Reporter, Deadline Hollywood, etc. . . .*). Article after article about how your competitors are making millions and winning award after award. On one hand, it's important to be knowledgeable about the economics and trends in your marketplace. On the other hand, it can be debilitating to count all of the money and kudos your competitors are receiving while you continue to slave away. Don't

---

2. A variation on Andrew Carnegie's "All honor's wounds are self-inflicted."

allow yourself to become a prisoner of envy. It saps your energy and impairs your objectivity. To hell with everyone else. Put on those envy blinders when analyzing the fact pattern in front of you. Look straight ahead, determine what makes sense for your deal and start running.

ELIMINATE LUST: THE DANGER OF WANTING

"Lust is to the other passions what the nervous fluid is to life; it supports them all, lends strength to them all. Ambition, cruelty, avarice, revenge are all founded on lust."

—Marquis de Sade

I make a distinction between eliminating envy and the related task of eliminating lust. Eliminating envy is about shaving away the excessive focus on others, what others have, what others do. Eliminating lust is the exercise of shaving away what we long for, what we desire. Our lusts may be completely reasonable but must be temporarily set aside. Otherwise, it may interfere with our dispassionate analysis and can lead to the tactical error of "wanting."

I learned a great lesson about wanting one Halloween when I was an undergraduate at UC Berkeley aka Cal. That year Halloween fell on a weekday, and there wasn't too much going on. Because I'm a big nerd, I decided to break out my Wolverine costume (old school comic book Wolverine, not hip and handsome Hugh Jackman Wolverine) and go trick-or-treating on Telegraph Avenue, the main street that has the local businesses frequented by the undergrads. Keep in mind, I was the only person in costume roaming the streets of Cal that evening. Perhaps, the other students were going to party it up over the weekend. With pillowcase in hand, I went from coffee house to donut shop to taco joint to hamburger stand in my gold and blue unitard, plastic Wolverine claws and mask bellowing, "Trick or Treat!" Amazingly, it was hugely successful. Perhaps, because they were completely surprised (or maybe they just took pity on the weird kid in the unitard), I hit the jackpot! Free biscotti and french fries and bear claws, oh my! I couldn't believe my good fortune. High on my fantastic haul, I stopped by Top Dog, Cal's favorite hot dog stand on my way back to the dorm. I confidently walked up to the counter in front of the grill to stake my claim. "Trick or Treat!" . . . nothing.

I waited a bit and repeated my demand . . . "Trick or Treat!" . . . nothing.

The man scraping the grill with his spatula didn't even pause from his duties to acknowledge me. Trust me, he definitely heard me. This place is literally 10 feet wide by 15 feet deep. Flummoxed and overconfident from my earlier success that evening, I clumsily stuttered, "I, I . . . want a hot dog."

The grill man paused from his scraping, slowly turned his head toward me and calmly stated, "It's good to want things."

He then turned back to continue his grill related duties.

Crestfallen, the mighty Wolverine left Top Dog and slunk back to his dorm room to solitarily gorge upon his Halloween treats. Halloween treats that did NOT include a hot dog from Top Dog, mind you.

I never forgot that moment. Something about the subtle disgust in his voice when he said: *"It's good to want things."* It stuck. I wanted a free hot dog. He did not want to give me a free hot dog. The world is not obliged to bend over backward so I can have what I want.

"Wanting" exists as a tactical error in the world of chess as well. It's when a player wants a particular strategic maneuver to work so much that they begin to lose touch with the big picture of the game. They are so focused on taking that bishop that they become oblivious to the checkmate headed their way in three moves.

The Top Dog guy was right. It is good to want things. Wanting things propels us to act. The problem is when your desired outcome clouds the objectivity of your analysis, making you oblivious to the checkmate coming your way in three moves.

ELIMINATE ANGER: THE TEMPORARY MADNESS

"He who angers you conquers you."

—**Elizabeth Kenny**

Dealmaking is combat. In combat people punch you in the face. Opponents are actively working against your interests. Anger is a natural reaction to people attempting or perhaps succeeding at kicking you in the groin. However, in order to see things as they are, Anger must be shaved away. The Roman poet Horace said: *"Anger is a short madness."* We can't allow madness to interfere with our cold calculations.

When you allow someone to anger you, you give them your power. Yes, someone wants to hurt you. That's ok. They perceive it to be in their best interest to do so. They will learn soon enough that it is not. Breathe. Count to 10, count to 100. Take a walk. You are a dealmaker, you cannot be rattled. You conquer. You will not be conquered.

ELIMINATE MORALITY: RISE ABOVE YOUR PRINCIPLES

"When a fellow says, 'It ain't the money but the principle of the thing,' it's the money."

—Kin Hubbard

A law school professor of mine told this fantastic story of when he was representing one side in a contentious show business labor dispute. The negotiation between the two sides was dragging on, and tensions were high. If the parties could not agree, there would be a strike, which would have significant economic impact to the entertainment industry. At a critical juncture, talks broke down. It looked like a debilitating strike would be eminent. My professor's frustrated client came to him and said, *"It's not right. We can't agree to these terms on principle!"*

My professor calmly responded, "Sometimes, you must rise above your principles."

His client took the deal. The strike was averted. Everyone made money.

It's natural to get emotionally involved in our work from a moral perspective, to feel earnestly that it's not fair how our client is being treated by the opposing party. That it's not right. The raw greed makes us queasy. The unfettered, unapologetic exploitation of people for money. But, this impulse to view things from a moral perspective must be shaved away when processing the information in front of us. We are dealmakers, not priests. We must rise above our principles.

INTELLECTUAL FREEDOM

"Only as you do know yourself can your brain serve you as a sharp and efficient tool. Know your own failings, passions, and prejudices so you can separate them from what you see."

—Bernard Baruch

Reality, it's all around us. We just have to be open to receiving it. How beautiful to train yourself to quietly, honestly, dispassionately observe the world around you. Passive, still, open to truth.

Dealmaking is a very complex and very human endeavor. You are dealing with hopes and fears and power and money and freedom. You are dealing with people's lives and the lives of their families. But, throughout this process, we must be able to maintain intellectual perspective. We must maintain objectivity in order to help our clients and collaborators make the right choices. By shaving away pride and envy and lust and anger and morality, we open our minds to unfettered critical thinking and the potential of achieving true intellectual freedom.

Sir Francis Bacon famously wrote, "Knowledge is power." I very much agree. But, if we twist and distort and subvert knowledge to comport with our own preconceived notions and desires, it loses its power and thus, we lose ours.

DUPLICITY'S DANGERS

"No man has a good enough memory to be a successful liar."
—**Abraham Lincoln**

Dealmaker's Commandment IV: Things Are Precisely as They Seem begs the question: What about deception? Surprisingly, the danger of deceiving yourself is usually far greater than the danger of being deceived by others. Let's look at this issue first from the perspective of the one doing the lying and then from the perspective from the one being lied to.

Overt lying as a tactic is overrated. There are too many moving parts to a successful lie; the machine can't help but break. First, everyone on your side needs to commit to the deception and not let the cat out of the bag. This is no small task. As Ben Franklin said: *"Three may keep a secret, if two of them are dead."*

Second, everyone on the opposing side needs to buy the ruse. We live in the Information Age. Our economy and culture are based upon the idea that everyone should have access to as much information as possible at all times. In addition to digital resources, you have contacts throughout your particular industry where you get information, as does the opposing side. Given the increasing ubiquity of information and the interconnectedness of people through social media platforms, good luck hiding the ball for long.

Third, let's say the machine holds and the lie successfully deceives the other side and the deal is closed. What are the odds that the truth never comes out? There are no secrets in Hollywood.

Whether it's on E! or *The National Enquirer* or *TMZ* or at a boozy industry cocktail party, the truth comes out. And then?

Then, you have lost credibility as a dealmaker. We are repeat players. You will see the same opponents again and again. In the next fight you are hobbled by the reputation of being a liar. Your word is your bond, and now that bond is worth pennies on the dollar. Not being able to give your word and have it stick is a strategic disadvantage that does stick.

Now, let's look at the other side of the coin. How do we deal with duplicity from the opposing side? My methodology to block subterfuge involves the following three steps: **The Smell Test, Due Diligence** and **Codification.**

- **The Smell Test**—In trial attorney Gerry Spence's excellent book, *How to Argue & Win Every Time*, he states that the truth is always the best argument because we recognize it instantly. He believes that there is a "biological advantage" to using the truth. As previously discussed, evolutionarily we are wired for fear as a method to promote self-preservation. Being deceived is dangerous, and we constantly scan our world for danger. Many times when someone lies to you, something seems off. It's difficult to put your finger on it, but it's there. A slight hesitation of speech. The way someone's eyes dart around the room. Perhaps, the piece of information they are putting forth does not comport with your experience in the marketplace. Something smells fishy. Sometimes this initial reaction is called "The Smell Test." It's like Spider Sense for dealmakers. Step one to block subterfuge is to ask, "Does this pass the Smell Test?"
- **Due Diligence**—Due Diligence is a fancy legal way of saying dig through a company's records to make sure they are not lying to you. If a dealmaker is not doing thorough due diligence, they are not doing their job. This is why it is important not to be rushed in closing a transaction. That's when mistakes happen. It's like getting married after the first date. If the other side is trying to compel you to complete due diligence in an unreasonably short amount of time or if they are being squirrelly about providing you information that you need, it's a major red flag.
- **Codification**—You need things in writing for a reason. To make sure that nobody gets cute. There is even a legal principle referred to as "The Statute of Frauds," which mandates that once a contract exceeds a certain dollar amount an oral agreement is not enforceable.

In part, because of my background as a child actor, I love the importance of the written contract in show business. The entertainment industry has developed blowing smoke into a high art form. Everybody loves your work. Everybody thinks you're great. There are more award ceremonies and kudos and honors than you can shake a Golden Globe at. But, the written contract reveals all. Between the four corners of each page is truth. The cold, hard, beautiful truth.

How much are you really worth to the studio? How real is your profit participation in the film? If there is a sequel, are you locked to continue your role? What is your piece of the merchandising?

Not only is the contract truth but the contract is power. There are mechanisms to keep the other side honest. Placing money in escrow to make sure the buyer doesn't welch. Auditing provisions to make sure the accounting is on the up and up. "Liquidated Damages" provisions that apply automatic financial penalties for contractual breach.

Between **The Smell Test, Due Diligence** and **Codification** the odds are very much stacked against overt deception as an effective tactic for repeat players.

QUESTION FOR SELF-MASTERY

DO I HAVE A SCARCITY MENTALITY OR AN ABUNDANCE MENTALITY?

"If you look at what you have in life, you'll always have more. If you look at what you don't have in life, you'll never have enough."
—Oprah Winfrey

When you observe the world around you, ask yourself, "Do I have a scarcity mentality or an abundance mentality?" A person with a scarcity mentality views the world as if it is a "zero sum game." If a competitor makes money, then there is less money for them to make. It harkens back to the ancient economic theory of mercantilism, which argued that a country could only measure it's wealth by the amount of gold bullion the king had locked up in his treasury. In all trade between countries, the side that got the most gold won. The other side lost.

In the late eighteenth century, economist Adam Smith debunked this mercantilist, scarcity mentality in his masterpiece *The Wealth of Nations.* He argued that both sides of a trade can win. One side trades gold for wine, because they really want some wine. The other side trades wine for gold, because they really want some gold. Both sides are better off and happier after the trade. This is an abundance mentality, aka "Let's all get rich together!"

When someone with a scarcity mentality discovers that a competitor has just signed a rich digital content deal, their reaction is, "Damn, now there is less money floating around the marketplace for me . . ." A person with an abundance mentality views the same piece of information and says, "Wow, my competitor made a lot of money with that digital deal! That market is really growing. I should be on the lookout for opportunities in that space."

Of course, there are certain circumstances when having a scarcity mentality is appropriate. Perhaps, there is only a certain amount of money in the budget of a film to allocate as producing fees to be split among three producers. In that case, there is a scarce amount of resources, and having a scarcity mentality is necessary and reasonable for purposes of negotiating the transaction.

However, having an abundance mentality as a default allows one to see opportunities and helps prevent envy from negatively impacting your own interests. If you find that you generally view the world from a scarcity mentality, try giving an abundance mentality a try. You might find that it automatically shifts your energy away from what others are doing and toward what you are doing—a far superior use of your resources.

OUR JOURNEY THUS FAR . . .

DEALMAKER'S COMMANDMENT I: IT IS BETTER TO BE FEARED THAN LOVED.

Being feared is more useful and reliable than being loved.

DEALMAKER'S COMMANDMENT II: POWER LEADS; REASON FOLLOWS.

Power, not reason, drives the outcome of a transaction.

DEALMAKER'S COMMANDMENT III: EVERYONE IS ON THE SAME SIDE . . . THEIR OWN.

Parties are motivated by and can be predicted to behave in accordance with their perceived best self-interest.

DEALMAKER'S COMMANDMENT IV: THINGS ARE PRECISELY AS THEY SEEM.

All manner of irrational and emotional impulses must be shaved away to objectively analyze the battlefield.

Now, the importance of opponent selection.

DEALMAKER'S COMMANDMENT V: NO PIG WRESTLING.

Bacon's always tempting, but not great for your cholesterol.

NO PIG WRESTLING

"Never wrestle with pigs. You both get dirty and the pig likes it."

—GEORGE BERNARD SHAW

COMBAT IS HONOR

"They say you're judged by the strength of your enemies."
—James Bond/*Quantum of Solace*

Knights don't joust against squires. CEOs don't negotiate against interns. Major League teams don't play Little League squads. The champ doesn't fight an unranked opponent. Unless you're Apollo Creed fighting Rocky, which did not turn out awesome for Apollo in *Rocky II* . . .

When you engage in combat with an opponent, you are bestowing honor upon them.[1] Combat is an exercise of equals. As you rise to higher and higher heights as a dealmaker, there are more and more pigs who would love to get a piece of you. Don't let them engage. Don't give those little filthy piggies an angle. They desperately want to get a shot at the champ. To sap your resources, to raise their reputation at the expense of yours. Don't help that pig become a prince. Discretion is very much the better part of valor.

A fundamental through line of the *Dealmaker's Ten Commandments* is gaining and maintaining control. To the fullest extent possible, we must control who our enemies are and the battles we fight with them. Sometimes, however, combat is thrust upon us, and we do not have a choice. Then we must use our resources to shape our enemy and the alter conditions of victory to our favor.

COMBAT IS EXPENSIVE

"Agree for the law is costly."

—William Camden

Nothing consumes a dealmaker's resources as greedily as combat. On an infinitely larger scale, think about real war. World War I, World War II, the Vietnam War, the Iraq War. Trillions of dollars spent; innumerable lives lost. One can be in favor of a particular war or against it, but the enormous cost of war is beyond debate. On a smaller scale, think of the costs associated with litigation or a labor strike or a mutually destructive price war among competitors. Dealmakers are instruments of capitalism. Successful capitalism is the art and science of best allocating resources to

---

1. Chris Matthews deals nicely with this topic in *Life Is a Campaign*.

achieve defined objectives. To impulsively engage in combat without a thorough analysis of the costs and benefits is clumsy capitalism and poor dealmaking. You must ascertain how much time, energy and capital this conflict is going to cost. Is it worth the resources? What about the opportunity cost? Is there a better use for your precious time and energy than this fight? Are you being compensated appropriately given the nature of the enemy and scope of the battle?

Combat can be costly to your reputation as well. As Mark Twain said: *"Never argue with a fool, onlookers may not be able to tell the difference."* The fog of war confuses both participant and observer. And there very well could be observers; nothing draws a crowd like a fight. Will wrestling that pig in front on this growing mass of onlookers lower your standing in your industry? Media outlets love to write about fights, because people love to read about fights—the more vindictive the better. "Pig wrestles pig! Read all about it!" When you throw that punch, the world may be watching and judging.

CHOOSE THE RIGHT ENEMY

"A man cannot be too careful in his choice of enemies."
—Oscar Wilde

Thomas Jefferson vs. John Adams. Abraham Lincoln vs. Stephen Douglas. Ronald Reagan vs. Tip O'Neal. Steve Jobs vs. Bill Gates. Elliot Ness vs. Al Capone. Jake LaMotta vs. Sugar Ray Robinson. Magic Johnson vs. Larry Bird. Luke Skywalker vs. Darth Vader. Hulk Hogan vs. "Rowdy" Roddy Piper. Vampires vs. Werewolves. Kramer vs. Kramer, and the list goes on.

The right enemy is a thing of beauty. How romantic to engage in combat with a worthy foe. The competition tests the limits of our intellect, ability and fortitude. It captures the imagination and can transform the combatants into legend. You need a worthy opponent to be considered a worthy competitor. Although there is no fixed formula, here are some things to keep in mind when evaluating a potential foe.

THE WRONG ENEMY

When deciding if someone is the wrong enemy, I start with some wisdom from Julius Caesar: *"It is not these well fed long haired men I fear, but the pale and hungry looking."* Tangling with someone who has no stature in your industry, nothing to lose and a ferocious desire to make a name for themselves is probably the worst type of enemy you could invent. This is quintessential pig wrestling. If you destroy them in the fight, your reputation does not improve. Additionally, the prize purse for the transaction is likely to be small. Thus, your economic upside is limited. Conversely, the downside risk to your reputation is huge. What if for some reason this kid takes you out? Perhaps it has nothing to do with your abilities. Perhaps your client has some drastic change of heart about their position on a deal. Perhaps, macroeconomic conditions impacting the deal shift suddenly. Then you just wrestled a pig and lost. Nobody wants to hear why you lost. It doesn't matter. You just got pinned by a pig. And even if you win, what if the win is not decisive enough? What if it's too decisive and you come off looking like a bullying jerk? Unlimited downside risk *and* limited upside reward? No thanks! Not a worthy foe.

THE RIGHT ENEMY

When deciding if someone is the right enemy, let's start with some wisdom from Baltasar Gracián: *"A wise man gets more use from his enemies than a fool from his friends."* What use can we get from a good enemy? It's somewhat the reverse of the Wrong Enemy analysis. We want to fight someone with greater stature then we have. If you lose, well, you fought the good fight against a larger opponent. If you win or tie, your rep increases. Significant potential upside with limited downside. Additionally, by fighting a better opponent, you can learn new moves and tactics by observing them during the battle. This is a key reason why opponent selection is so important. Magic Johnson never could have been as good without having to up his game to compete with Larry Byrd. Abraham Lincoln must have become a stronger orator after the hours and hours he spent in public debate with Stephen Douglas.

A good enemy shows you where you need to improve. Great, now you know! Fix it and evolve into a stronger competitor. A note of caution, however. Beware of fighting an enemy much larger than you unless the battle conditions are just perfect. Opponent selection is an exercise in consistent, incremental improvement, not suicide.

CHOOSE THE RIGHT BATTLE

"There is no instance of a country have benefitted from a prolonged warfare."

—**Sun Tzu**

You have found a worthy opponent and are eager to demonstrate your prowess to the marketplace. But, choosing the right enemy is not sufficient. You must choose the right battle as well. You're not Don Quixote tilting at windmills. You want a fight you can win. So given the inherently messy nature of combat, how does a dealmaker know when combat is appropriate? To analyze the likelihood of victory, I perform a **Gun/Ammo/Target Analysis** or **GAT-NALYSIS** if you are feeling cheeky.

GAT-NALYSIS

"Only a fool fights a battle he knows he cannot win."

—Genghis Khan

I have shortened Gun/Ammo/Target to GAT, because, according to all of the gangster rap I have listened to, 'GAT' is a really cool slang word for gun. Also, please note that the only gun I have ever fired is the one that came with my Nintendo Entertainment System to play "Duck Hunt." So please forgive me if my gun-related analogies below are not scientifically accurate.

GUN

Your leverage in the specific deal is the "Gun." If I represent an actor who is the irreplaceable and beloved star of a very successful television series, perhaps my gun is an awesome high powered AK-47 or a sweet gigantic bazooka. Contrarily, if I am representing the fourth lead of the same television series and the producers consider that actor replaceable, my gun might be a measly sling shot. Once I know what my weapon is, the second question is what is my ammunition?

AMMO

My client's resolve/fortitude regarding the deal is the "Ammo." If the client is determined to get the big bucks under any circumstances, even at the expense of the deal going away, my ammo is powerful. The lead actor of the series has so many other offers pouring in for cool projects that the only way continuing his role on the series is interesting to him is if he is making beaucoup bucks. He is completely comfortable with walking away from the deal if his demands are not met. In that case my ammo is a high-tech, armor-piercing, adamantium-coated instrument of destruction. My gun is an AK–47, and my bullets are strong. We are in good shape so far.

But, what if the lead actor feels that, from a creative standpoint, being in the series is very important for his career. Perhaps, he is working on other projects with the producers on the show and doesn't want to make waves with an acrimonious negotiation. My client's perspective can be extremely appropriate and reasonable, however, my bullets are not armor piercing. My bullets are now made from Styrofoam. I have a tons of leverage (a great gun), but the client lacks the will to fight (i.e., Styrofoam bullets). I come in to jack up his rate. The producers give me sufficient pushback. The client will choose to fold.

How about the actor who is the fourth lead? He may be completely adamant about getting a huge raise regardless of the circumstances. My bullets are strong, but my weapon is a sling shot. Can't do much damage with a sling shot regardless of the ammo. What if this actor's will is weak? Then my bullets are Styrofoam. I can do even less damage using Styrofoam bullets for the slingshot. Slingshot with hollow points/slingshot with Styrofoam: either way it's not looking good. The final piece of the GAT-NALYSIS is target.

TARGET

What is my target? What are the parameters for a successful outcome to the negotiation, the conditions for victory? If success is considered increasing the actor's salary by a modest 10 percent, then my target is large and five feet away. If success is considered increasing the actor's salary to ten times what it currently is, then my target is small and 500 feet away.

I look down at the gun I am wielding. I feel the ammo as I put the bullets into the clip. I squint at my target. How likely am I to make this shot? GAT-NALYSIS

REDEFINE THE WRONG ENEMY

"I'm not looking at you dudes, I'm look'n past you."

—Jay Z

Unfortunately, we cannot always choose our enemies. Sometimes they are thrust upon us. But, we still have options. Being a great dealmaker is about control. If we cannot control who our enemy is, perhaps we can control how they are defined. We have tools to shape them.

MINIONS

One of my favorites is the skillful use of minions. If you are fortunate enough to have subordinates, you can fully engage the enemy in combat without giving them the honor of engaging them in combat. Disempower your enemy by not responding to their calls or e-mails. They call you, but they get a return call from your lieutenant. They are not on your level; they do not have the privilege of speaking to you. However, they do receive the privilege of getting clocked by the full force of your negotiating power as administered through the vessel of your associate. Provide your enemy with an all risk/no reward scenario. If they win, they have bested your junior. No glory in that. If they lose, they have lost to your junior. Shameful . . . maybe they've lost a step.

KILL THEM WITH KINDNESS

This one seems radical, I know. You don't have to believe me, but believe Abe Lincoln who said *"Do I not destroy my enemies when I make them my friends."* In certain cases, you can destroy an enemy by fostering a mutually beneficial and collaborative relationship. This is helpful when you are fighting opponents with great stature but you lack the battle conditions for a favorable GAT-NALYSIS. Perhaps, you are negotiating against a wise old lion, a silverback gorilla. An aging but powerful opponent who has already made their mark with nothing further to prove. Neutralize this opponent by appealing to their vanity and exhaustion. Be friendly to them. Give them the deference they are due. Discuss various unrelated transactions they have done that have influenced you. Be a fan. Perhaps, you genuinely are. They don't want a big fight but will provide one if needlessly provoked. Don't poke the lion. Be cool. Improve the terms as much as possible without all out Armageddon. Live to fight another day.

STAY ABOVE THE MUD

When an industry peer goads you about an annoying competitor in the marketplace who you would love to see hit by a bus, just smile and say: *"Bob's great. Doing some great work right now."* Make sure you say it sincerely. As George Burns said, *"The key to success is sincerity. If you can fake that you've got it made . . ."* By giving your competitor their due, you elevate your own stature. It shows that you are much too powerful to be threatened by this gnat. It also will drive your competitor nuts when it gets back to them. So, that's a secondary benefit as well.

REDEFINE THE WRONG BATTLE'S CONDITIONS FOR VICTORY

"Victory is no longer a truth. It is only a word to describe who is left alive in the ruins."

—Lyndon B. Johnson

Perhaps a battle that is inherently a real loser is thrust upon us. What then? Let's perform our trusty GAT-NALYSIS and see what we can tweak.

It is difficult and sometimes inappropriate to attempt to influence the **Gun** (intrinsic deal leverage) and/or **Ammo** (the client's will to fight). However, it is much easier and sometimes highly appropriate to adjust the **Target** (conditions for a successful transactional outcome).

Perhaps, the client has unreasonable expectations regarding the transactions. A tiny target that's far away. Educate the client with the precedent of other deals in the space. Manage your side's expectations. Bring the target closer in line with market conditions. Perhaps, there are additional long-term goals that can be achieved in future negotiations by "setting the table" with this negotiation. Even if the current round of negotiations is not successful, you have signaled to the other side that they will need to open their checkbook next season when your client's popularity has increased. More cache = more cash. Perhaps, there are things other than upfront compensation that would benefit your client that the opposing side will more willingly concede to (i.e., reduced exclusivity, better perks, a bump in title, a bonus if certain viewer ratings are hit). Baby steps, progress. Creating a better jumping off point for next year's negotiations. Get creative to increase the size of the target. With some diligence you may be able to favorably alter the preset conditions for victory, in effect bringing your target closer and making it larger.

THE MOST WORTHY ENEMY OF ALL

"Yet is every man his greatest enemy, and, as it were, his own executioner."

—Thomas Browne

Billy Conn aka "The Pittsburgh Kid" fought for the Heavyweight Boxing Championship against the mighty Joe Louis aka "The Brown Bomber" in 1941. Billy was the current Light Heavyweight Champion but gave up his belt to have a shot at Joe. Amazingly, he did so without going up in weight. Joe Louis outweighed him by 25 pounds at the time of the fight. That's absurd on its face. What's even more absurd is that the smaller and more mobile Billy Conn had a secure lead on points after the 12th round of a 15-round bout. Billy would hit Joe Louis and run around the ring, exhausting his much larger opponent. Inexplicably, between the 12th and 13th round, Billy decided he wanted to knock out the champ. His corner begged him to continue to dance for three rounds and win on points.

Ding-Ding! Round 13 begins! Billy stops dancing, squares up directly in front of the Brown Bomber and . . . gets knocked the hell out. Fight's over. Joe Louis retains his championship and goes on to become one of the greatest boxers of all time. After the fight in his locker room, a perplexed reporter asked the Pittsburgh Kid why he went for the knockout. Billy Conn looked up at the reporter and said, *"I lost my head and a million bucks . . . What's the use of being Irish if you can't be stupid?"*

Being half Irish, I very much appreciate that story. I have done some really stupid stuff in my day, but I imagine we all have. Self-sabotage is a hell of a thing. Just as we are in the best position of anyone on the planet to impact our behavior in a positive manner, we are also in the best position of anyone on the planet to impact our behavior in a destructive manner. I've thought about self-sabotage quite a bit. How could Richard Nixon be the most powerful man in the world but be so insecure and paranoid as to bug his own phones, sowing the seed for his own resignation? How can professional athletes make millions upon millions only to squander it all away on nonsense? How can successful artists with everything that life has to offer at their fingertips wind up destitute after destroying their own gifts in a haze of substance abuse?

Part of it is that we are all subject to human appetites and frailties. There is also mental illness, of course. But, self-sabotage is a powerful recurring force of its own. I'm not a psychologist, so feel free to completely disagree with and disregard my thoughts on this matter. My experience is not academic, but anecdotal. It's based on what I have seen happen to certain clients and friends and foes over the years. I think that our perception of ourselves on the inside, however it was formed, is dominant. If we feel unattractive or impoverished or dumb on the inside, we listen to that voice. Even if what the outside world is telling us is completely different. You can be a multimillionaire but still feel broke. You can be an Adonis and still feel fat. You can be a genius but still feel like an idiot.

Self-sabotage is that inside voice creating equilibrium between our inside world and the outside world. If our inside voice feels that we are poor, it will make sure that we blow our fortune so that we are poor in our inside world and the outside world. If our inside voice feels we are weak, it will make sure that we squander our power so that we are helpless inside and out.

Don't be a victim of self-sabotage and become your own worst enemy. Why snatch defeat from the jaws of victory? If you beat yourself, then you deprive the world of the chance of kicking your ass. Now, that's not very sporting at all.

QUIET THE SOUL? GIVE IT A GOAL!

> *"Nothing contributes so much to tranquilize the mind as a steady purpose—a point on which the soul can fix its intellectual eye."*
> **—Mary Shelley**

How then to avoid self-sabotage and move beyond self-doubt and anxiety? My personal panacea is goal setting. Need to quiet your soul? Well, give it a goal! There is no substitute. Something about having a concrete, achievable goal in your mind's eye is magic. It focuses energy that could be used for self-destructive or wasteful behavior and creates an opportunity for progress, to improve your abilities and your station. Goals free you from the shadowy prison of the mind. They save you from "Why?" and "What if?" and bring you into the light of the world, the here and now. Goals are growth, and growth is life.

TRANSCEND STATUS THREATS

> *"Comparison is the thief of joy"*
> **—Thodore Roosevelt**

When an unworthy foe threatens your status to goad you into pig wrestling, don't take the bait. Status threats are a remarkable waste of time, energy and life. They are also remarkably human. They have done experiments, observing how the brain responds when a person's status is threatened.[2] The response is very similar to when a person feels physical pain. When you are embarrassed

---

2. Please see David Rock's excellent book, *Your Brain at Work*, for further discussion.

in front of your peers, it actually hurts; your brain registers pain. This may seem crazy, but scientists have theorized that our strong response to status threats have a reasonable basis in the evolution of early man.

Back in the caveman days, if your status in the village was low, you might actually die. The hunters are important and have status. The fertile females have status. The wise village mystic who can speak to the gods has status. But the clumsy weakling who isn't pulling his or her weight and making a contribution to the success of the village does not have status. If the hunt is unsuccessful and there is not enough food to go around, guess who goes hungry? Having low status could be hazardous to your health. No wonder it hurt when I showed up to the senior prom in an '81 Plymouth Reliant.

With this idea in mind, think of how many meetings you have attended and banal conversations you have had that are rife with status threat related chatter. Name dropping, conspicuous consumption, endless bragging and posturing. And what is the reason for this idiotic exercise? Our caveman doesn't want to be last in line when the hunt comes up short. It hurts to run into your ex-wife's new boyfriend at the game and see that he has better seats than you. It's exhilarating to have a better car than your neighbor. I'm rolling in a Corvette; no way I'm gonna starve!

Beware of the impact of status threats to you and those around you. Once you're conscience of the prevalence of status threat related behavior, it makes observing it seem somewhat comical. My solution? I go back to Andy Warhol's advice. You drive a Lamborghini, so what? Your great-great grandpappy came over on the Mayflower, so what? You live in a ginormous house that you can barely make the payments on, so what?

Mind your knitting. Focus on things that matter to you because they matter to you, not because you can brag about them to strangers and frenemies. Tell your inner caveman that there is plenty of food to go around. He is not going to starve.

QUESTION FOR SELF-MASTERY

WHAT KIND OF ENEMY AM I?

"One does not hate as long as one has a low esteem of someone, but only when one esteems him to be an equal or superior."
—Friedrich Nietzsche

If your opponent hates you, it means you are probably doing something right. Keep up the good work! We have talked quite a bit about choosing and shaping your enemy, but what about how your opponents will be choosing and attempting to shape you? Ask yourself, "What kind of enemy am I?"

As a dealmaker you create a deal persona, your style of play. Of course, you must vary your tactics depending on the battle, but generally how do you play the game? For constructing your deal persona, allow me to use a poker analogy. In traditional poker theory, you can be a "loose" player or a "tight" player. A loose player will stay in the game with a lot of hands. A tight player will only play with higher quality hands. Additionally, your style can be "aggressive" or "weak." An aggressive player will bet and raise aggressively when they feel they have the best hand. A weak player is more likely to call another's bet than bet themselves. Thus there are four classical styles of play: Tight/Aggressive, Tight/Weak, Loose/Aggressive, Loose/Weak.

When you are playing poker, the opponent you hate to play against is the one who is Tight/Aggressive. It's hard to get their money because they are not going to risk their chips when their odds are not favorable. If you stay in until the end of the hand hoping to catch a lucky card, they are going to make you pay. If you don't catch that flush, it's gonna cost you.

When choosing your deal persona, I suggest Tight/Aggressive. Be prudent, play conservatively. But, when you have the advantage, hit them hard, make them pay. Then rinse and repeat. Just because your stack of chips has grown, you should not shift your style from tight to loose. Don't let them win their chips back by getting sloppy. Stay Tight/Aggressive. Make them hate you. Be the player that you would never want to play against. Choosing your deal persona is the one time it actually does make sense to be your own worst enemy.

OUR JOURNEY THUS FAR . . .

DEALMAKER'S COMMANDMENT I: IT IS BETTER TO BE FEARED THAN LOVED.

Being feared is more useful and reliable than being loved.

DEALMAKER'S COMMANDMENT II: POWER LEADS; REASON FOLLOWS.

Power, not reason, drives the outcome of a transaction.

DEALMAKER'S COMMANDMENT III: EVERYONE IS ON THE SAME SIDE . . . THEIR OWN.

Parties are motivated by and can be predicted to behave in accordance with their perceived best self-interest.

DEALMAKER'S COMMANDMENT IV: THINGS ARE PRECISELY AS THEY SEEM.

All manner of irrational and emotional impulses must be shaved away to objectively analyze the battlefield.

DEALMAKER'S COMMANDMENT V: NO PIG WRESTLING.

Combat is honor. Choose your enemies and battles wisely. If combat is thrust upon you, choose to define your enemy and the conditions for victory.

Now, to the dance!

DEALMAKER'S COMMANDMENT VI: TAKE YES FOR YES, MAYBE FOR YES AND NO FOR MAYBE.

The rhythm of the negotiation beckons . . .

TAKE YES FOR YES, MAYBE FOR YES AND NO FOR MAYBE

"What's mine is mine and what's yours is negotiable."

—JOHN F. KENNEDY[1]

CHAPTER OUTLINE

Negotiation Is Dance

Yes for Yes, Maybe for Yes and No for Maybe

Tempo

Fancy Steps

Strobe Lights and Disco Balls

---

1. Used ironically by Kennedy. Full quote is "We cannot negotiate with people who say 'What's mine is mine and what's yours is negotiable.'"

NEGOTIATION IS DANCE

"The man who can't dance thinks the band is no good."
—Polish Proverb

One two three. One two three. One two three. That's a waltz.

One two, one two three. One two, one two three. One two, one two three. That's a cha cha.

Offer, counter, close. Offer, counter, close. Offer, counter, close. That's a deal.

A negotiation is a dance. Each one has its own rhythm and tonality. The tempo changes as momentum increases or decreases. If you control the song being played, you are the maestro. If you are controlled by the song being played you are the backup triangle player. To make the analogy millennial appropriate, if you control the rhythm, you are the DJ. If you are controlled by the rhythm, you are probably high out of your mind on "Molly." Whatever that is . . .

The basic steps of the Deal Dance are as simple as One, Two, Three:

(1) Party A makes a proposal
(2) Party B either:
  • Accepts the proposal. Deal closes, and dance is done.
  • Walks away (i.e., passes). No deal made, and dance is done.
  • Make a counter proposal. No deal made, but the dance continues. Go to step three.
(3) Party A can either:
  • Accept the counter proposal. Deal closes, and dance is done.
  • Walk away. No deal is made, and dance is done.
  • Make a counter to Party B's counter. No deal made, but the dance continues. Go back to Step two.

Pretty simple little ditty, right? The number of times the deal bounces back and forth is variable, but at its essence, dealmaking is simple. Offer, counter, close. One, two, three. Like a waltz. But, like most things involving money, power and human emotion, this dance can get pretty complex pretty quickly.

YES FOR YES, MAYBE FOR YES AND NO FOR MAYBE

"Dance is the only art of which we ourselves are the stuff of which it is made."

—Ted Shawn

Fred Astaire, the elegant and graceful film star of Hollywood's golden age, is considered by many to be the greatest popular dancer of all time. Effortlessly, he would glide and tap and spin. Nobody could pull off a tux and top hat like that dude. The secret is that even though he made it seem so easy, he was absolutely relentless in creating that "effortless" performance. He would rehearse a single scene for days. Eventually his dancing partner, Ginger Rogers, couldn't take the grueling schedule and quit. Fred Astaire did fine after that, being paired with leading ladies such as Cyd Charisse, Rita Hayworth and Audrey Hepburn.

Just like great dancers can transform a misstep into a twirl and a stumble into a graceful dip, great dealmakers can start with a "No," twirl that into a "Maybe," then gracefully dip that into a "Yes." And just like Fred Astaire, it takes a tremendous amount of practice. I'm going to show you the moves, but ultimately to become a great dealmaker you need practice. With sufficient experience you will recognize patterns, opportunities, traps and be able to adjust your moves accordingly.

Taking **Yes for Yes, Maybe for Yes and No for Maybe** is about choreographing a series of steps that have increasingly favorable outcomes for your side—positive momentum where the other guys are either on your boat or they're under it.

TAKE YES FOR YES

This seems beyond obvious, but you might be surprised at how easy it is to self-sabotage on this one. "Take Yes for Yes" means take your victory and bank it.

In sales, if you get the prospect to say "Yes, I'll buy it," you don't respond by saying "Are you sure?" No way! You say "Great! Sign right here." Followed by, "Hey, have you thought about buying a second one for the office?" Progress, momentum, victory.

TAKE MAYBE FOR YES

Taking Maybe for Yes could go something like this:

First Round

Me: "My client needs creative control over the script."

Other Side: "We've discussed that internally and we're not completely comfortable with that."

Second Round

Me: "I've spoken to my client and we are able to give you meaningful consultation on the script as long as my client has the final say."

Other Side: "Well, we don't feel that meaningful consultation gives us sufficient control over the script."

Third Round

Me: "So, my client gets creative control subject to your meaningful consultation, yes?"

Other Side: "Meaningful consultation doesn't give us sufficient control on our end."

Me: "No problem. Provide me with some language that works as long as my client has final say. Next issue . . ."

You may win on that issue, you may not. But you are pulling the other side from "Maybe" to "Yes." If it is possible to win on that issue, you will. Progress, momentum, victory.

TAKE NO FOR MAYBE

Taking No for Maybe could look like this:

First Round

Me: "We absolutely need creative control!"

Other Side: "No way in hell are we giving you creative control!"

Me: "I understand your position, let me discuss internally with my client."

Round Two

Me: "We need creative control."

Other Side: "No."

Round Three

Me: "We'd really like to have creative control."

Other Side: "No."

Round Four

Me: "Hey if you give my client creative control, we can finally close this thing."

Other Side: "We told you, no creative control. It's a total deal breaker on our side."

Me: "I understand. Well, if you can increase my client's profit participation in the film and make sure she is attached to sequels I can try to get my side to drop the request for creative control. I can't guarantee that we will accept, but I'll give it a shot."

Taking No for Maybe is an exercise in wearing down the opposition. You may be surprised, if their will is worn down sufficiently, they may actually give in. Maybe you get no concessions for giving up on the ask. But, you can be confident in telling your client that if creative control was a winnable point, you would have gotten it. Progress, momentum, victory.

TEMPO

"And those who were seen dancing were thought to be insane by those who could not hear the music."

—Friedrich Nietzsche

No one may be able to hear it except you, but each deal has its own tempo. A drum beat. Offer, counter, close. Boom, boom, boom. The tempo leads us to the deal's finale, either the deal makes or the deal breaks. Or perhaps it just floats out there partially open, partially closed. There are times when that is advantageous as well.

INCREASE THE TEMPO

There are myriad reasons you would want to speed up the tempo of the deal dance. Here are a few:

- Resistance is breaking down on the other side. You got 'em on the ropes. They are dazed and have begun to fight among themselves. You want to press the advantage. Pummel them into submission before they can regroup.
- You are negotiating a group of deals, but this one is the linchpin. If you are able to close this one, the others will fear that the train is leaving without them and immediately fall in line.

- You want to sell on the sizzle, not the steak. Your client is a director who has a film that is being released in two weeks. The film has a great deal of positive buzz (i.e., sizzle). You want to close a favorable deal for their next film while the buzz for the current film is still buzzing. When the current film is released the box office numbers tell the true tale; the sizzle becomes steak. If the numbers are great and confirm the sizzle, an open deal won't get much better. If the numbers are bad and counter the sizzle, an open deal will get much worse or potentially go away. Therefore, increase the tempo and close before the current film is released. Sell on the sizzle, not the steak.[2]

The simplest way to increase the tempo is to make sure that you respond to the other side immediately and through multiple methods of communications. They send you their comments to the contract on Monday. You immediately incorporate what comments you see fit and send back the amended agreement on Tuesday via e-mail cc'ing all of the relevant parties. This is followed up with a daily phone call to check on the status of their response. Sound annoying? It's supposed to be. The other side will want to close the deal just to get you off their phone sheet.

Perhaps the attorney you are negotiating against is not responding to the barrage? Fine, reach out to the agent or manager on the other side. Make it annoying to them as well.

Maybe that is not sufficient. Are you working with agents or managers on your side who can help bug the reps on the other side? Enlist them in the campaign.

Still not speeding things up. How about the "End Around"? Perhaps your client is a television producer trying to make a deal with an actor to star in their pilot. Have the producer go around the lawyer, agent and manager and use their personal relationship with the actor to speak directly to them. Producers are clever; they will likely be able to convey the need to speedily close the actor's deal. Then the actor reaches out to his or her own team and presses them to close the transaction. Now, the opposing lawyer is being pressured by the agent and manager on their side because the agent and manager are getting pressured by their client, the actor. The other side now has risk because their own client is dissatisfied. Risk equals fear. More and more, it is in everyone's perceived best self-interest to close this damn deal.

---

2. Producer Art Linson discussed this idea more fully in his excellent book *A Pound of Flesh: Perilous Tales of How to Produce Movies in Hollywood.*

Basically, if you want to increase the tempo, be a pain in the ass. Get creative! But, remember speeding things up does not give you the right to be sloppy. There is no excuse for not doing the appropriate due diligence and not properly vetting the contracts. If anything goes wrong, it's your ass. So get ready to put in some late nights.

DECREASE THE TEMPO

Why rush things? Take it easy, man! Relax. Haste makes waste and all that. There are plenty of reasons to slow things down as well:

- You want to wait to get the other side "a little bit pregnant." For example, you represent an actor in a film that is shooting in two weeks. You have worked out the major terms but are fighting over which costs can be deducted out of the profits of the film. You keep the deal open. Filming commences and they have no signed agreement with the lead actor in their film. Too late for the opposing side to threaten to get a replacement. Your actor is already on film, and they are "pregnant." Now, when you are working out the final details your leverage is immense.

- You are considering a few mutually exclusive deals at once. You need to wait for certain macroeconomic events to see which deal is the best to enter.

- You need more time to complete the proper due diligence for the transaction.

- You're not sure you want to be in business with the opposing side and want to see how they behave during the course of the negotiation. The protracted fight will bring out their true character.

- The opposing side is desperate to close quickly and stalling weakens their position. By the time they actually get you on the phone, they will accept any terms for fear of missing an important deadline without a deal in place.

- Being deliberate and taking your own sweet time shows strength. You can take the deal or leave it. You are playing hardball in order to achieve better terms.

- The opposing side is gaining momentum and you need to stop the charge.

Choice is powerful. Slowing things down allows you to keep your options open, which can be extremely useful. The obvious way to slow things down is to not return calls and e-mails. Be unavailable for meetings or teleconferences. Slow the drumbeat to your chosen tempo. Perhaps you respond to the other side ten days after receiving their counter offer instead of two.

The tricky aspects of slowing the tempo are **plausible deniability** and **internal communication**. Even though you are intentionally slowing things down, it is considered bad form and potentially bad faith to overtly do so. There must be plausible deniability. You're not intentionally slowing things down, you've been on vacation. You've been having some dental work done. You've been slammed with a new film you are working on. All reasonable excuses for your tardy response. The second important consideration is internal communication. When you slow things down, the other side will try all of the tactics mentioned above to speed things up (i.e., the end around, complaining to other reps on your team, etc . . .). The way to inoculate against this is solid internal communication. You must speak to the other members of your team and your client to explain the tactic. Then they are prepared when the opposing side approaches them directly. You never want your team to be surprised.

STOP THE MUSIC!

In certain circumstances stopping the dance entirely makes sense. When the music stops, the silence is deafening. Here are some ways to pull the plug on the jukebox.

THE POLITE PASS

The opposing side has made their proposal. Instead of accepting or making a counterproposal back, you do the unexpected. You say, "Thanks gang, we really appreciate the effort, but it looks like we are too far apart. Best of luck and hopefully we can figure something out on the next one." The dance is done. The party is over. You have passed. Because the pass was polite, you have left the door open for the other side to come back. If they do, they are dead. Coming back to the table after the other side has passed is admitting they are desperate to close the deal. They need you and as Benjamin Franklin said, *"Necessity never made a good bargain."*

Remember, if you pass you have to be prepared to really walk away from the deal. If it's just a bluff, the tables can easily be turned. You pass. They accept your pass. You come back to restart the negotiation. They smugly say "Wait, I thought you guys passed?" Your side is now toast. The other side may walk away on principal. They may make their new proposal worse than the previous proposal to teach you a lesson. Don't pull out a knife unless you're going to use it, and don't pass unless you are prepared to walk.

THE IMPOLITE PASS

This is basically the polite pass with four letter words. "You dirty #%$%#!!! This is complete #%$&! Forget this @#$&#! We are through here!" Depending on how filthy you get, it is unlikely that the other side will come back. You use the Impolite Pass to make a point. To punish their offensive proposal. To teach them not to waste your precious time.

But, if for some reason they do come back to the table after the Impolite Pass . . . oh brother! They are doomed. At that point it's a robbery. Open your bag and start filling it with their money.

PASS BY REVOCATION

There is a third type of pass, which does not happen often but does deserve mention. If you put forth an offer or counter, you can revoke the proposal before the other side counters, accepts or rejects. Perhaps, market conditions have changed and you no longer want to do the deal. Perhaps, the actor your producer was going to hire just had some terrible scandal come to light in the press. You no longer want to do the deal, so you revoke your proposal. The deal is dead, and the other side is angry. Pass by revocation does not allow the other side an opportunity to make a move. It may be necessary, but it will likely cause bad blood.

FANCY STEPS

> *"too clever by half: Shrewd but flawed by overthinking or excessive complexity, with a resulting tendency to be unreliable or unsuccessful."*
> **—wiktionary.org**

I love those "wedding dance gone wrong" clips on YouTube and America's Funniest Home Videos. The best man is hammered and tries to do some complex hip-hop move where he holds his left ankle with his right hand and tries to jump through the crease with his right leg. A lot needs to go right for that move to end in success. If any calculation is slightly off, to the horror of the wedding goers and the amusement of the viewers at home, he will totally bust his ass. There's a lesson here.

When doing your deal dance beware of making a move that is unnecessarily complex and risky aka "too clever by half." Here are some characteristics of moves that can easily fall into the too clever by half category:

- Moves that require any cooperation from the other side (i.e., the other side believes your lies and then behaves in the manner you think they will based upon believing those lies).
- Moves that require excessive cooperation on your own side (i.e., performing collective bargaining for a cast of actors when they are not similarly situated and the group will be unlikely to hold together).
- Moves that have a lot of moving parts. Machines with a lot of moving parts have more ways to break down and usually require perfect timing to function (i.e., anything that looks like a Rube Goldberg cartoon).

Watch the fancy moves, kiddo. Keep it simple, stupid!

STROBE LIGHTS AND DISCO BALLS

"If you can't convince them, confuse them."

—A. C. Wilson

Things can get pretty hazy out on the dance floor. Plenty of distractions at the club. Flashing lights. Loud music. Good look'n folks all around. Alcohol aplenty. Who the hell just spilled their drink on me?

Offer, counter, close.

Things get hazy in the heat of dealmaking as well. The other side trying to scare the hell out of your client. That they will sue them, bankrupt them if things don't work out. The media has suddenly taken an interest in your renegotiation. New salacious details released each day on the wonderful worldwide interweb. The other reps on your side are preparing their daggers to drive into your back just in case the deal goes south.

Offer, counter, close

Breathe in. Breathe out. Stay cool. Be smart. Don't be stupid. Be smart. It's not complex. It's simple.

No matter how convoluted the deal dance becomes, remember the steps. It's always the same. Offer, counter, close. Don't get distracted by the strobe lights and disco balls. Keep it simple. Where is the deal currently? We made the last counter. It's in the other side's court. Their turn. We don't get scared of their threats. We weather the storm in the media. We're cool like the Fonz. We don't get rattled. Their move: accept our counter proposal, make a counter to our counter proposal or pass. Everything else is noise.

The good news is that all that distracting club hubbub works both ways. Maybe you slip the waitress a C-note to buy them a round of shots and flirt with them while they're mulling over their next move . . .

NEVER NEGOTIATE AGAINST YOURSELF

"This deal is getting worse all the time."
—**Lando Calrissian**/*The Empire Strikes Back*

Quid pro quo. This for that. A simple idea but a fundamentally important one for dealmakers. When doing the deal dance, the other side desperately wants you to do something stupid. Negotiating against yourself is very stupid. Here's how it works:

> **Me:** We will hire your guy for $100K
> **Other Side:** That doesn't work for us.
> **Me:** What does work for you?
> **Other Side:** How high can you go?
> **Me:** $125K?
> **Other Side:** Still no good.
> **Me:** $150K, but that's as far we can go.
> **Other Side:** Still no good.
> **Me:** $175K?

You can see how this is going. Not awesome. You are negotiating against yourself. You have messed up the steps. When you make an offer they must accept, counter or pass. You come up a bit, they come down a bit. Quid pro quo. They must accept your proposal, tell you what number works for them or affirmatively walk away. If you negotiate against yourself you are allowing them to have the benefit of passing without taking the risk of passing. To hell with that. If $100K does not work on their end, fine. What number does? Negotiate against the other side, not yourself.

This begs the question, why not just cut the dance short by starting with your bottom-line figure? "$150K and that's it!" That's only is effective if you are willing to immediately walk away if they won't agree. When you say $150K, the other side thinks that your true bottom line is higher. Don't cancel the dance, why ruin everybody's fun?

HOW MANY STEPS AM I THINKING AHEAD?

"To see things in the seed, that is genius."

—Lao Tzu

When doing the deal dance and as an entrepreneur in general, you cannot only be thinking of the next move. Then you are reactive, you are being controlled by your opponent and the whims of fortune. You must be thinking three steps, four steps ahead. You must have the end game in mind in order to be proactive, in order to have control.

> *"David said, 'Do you know why every single start-up studio has failed over the last 55 years?' He said, 'Because they've been underfunded and we are going to overfund Dreamworks and that's the only way we have a snowball's chance in hell to survive.'"*
> **—Steven Spielberg discussing David Geffen**[3]

In the world of entertainment, it's hard to imagine someone who has been more steps ahead of the game than David Geffen. In 1969, he became a millionaire at 26 when he sold a music publishing company that he co-founded to CBS for $4.5 million. In 1970, he started Asylum Records signing some of the biggest acts of the 1970s, including The Eagles, Joni Mitchell, Bob Dylan, Linda Ronstadt and Jackson Browne. In 1972, he merged Asylum Records with Warner Communication's Elektra Records, becoming one of the largest shareholders of Warner Communications in the process. He ran Elektra/Asylum until being named Vice Chairman of the Warner Brothers Film Studios. He didn't love having a boss and resigned his position. In 1980, he founded Geffen Records, which signed such acts as Cher, John Lennon, Elton John and Guns 'N' Roses. In 1983, he founded the Geffen Film Company whose initial release was *Risky Business*—the film that made the then unknown Tom Cruise a star. He began financing/producing a number of stage productions including *Cats*, one of the longest running and most profitable musicals in

---

3. Quotes are from PBS's *American Masters: Inventing David Geffen*. A fantastic documentary, definitely worth watching.

Broadway history. In 1990, he sold Geffen Records to MCA in a deal that ultimately earned him upwards of $800 million. He became a billionaire shortly thereafter when Japanese conglomerate Matsushita made an all-cash acquisition of MCA.

In 1994 Geffen collaborated with Steven Spielberg and Jeffrey Katzenberg to form DreamWorks Studios, which brings us to Steven's quote above. Geffen was able to lock down $2 billion in cash and credit facilities to start up the studio. At the time, the industry "experts" felt that it was an absolutely absurd amount of money to fund the venture. Geffen felt otherwise.

"We were $1.8 billion invested before we started to turn a profit. Once again David's instincts were perfect."

—Jeffrey Katzenberg

They were $1.8 billion in the red until they turned the corner. Two-hundred million dollars remain on the line of credit. Geffen wasn't three steps ahead of everyone, he was ten steps ahead of everyone. He still is.

To be a great dealmaker it's not enough to know the dance, to execute the correct move or countermove. You have to predict where the deal is ultimately going and how it will get there each step of the way; to see the trajectory, the permutations, the possibilities without going mad. Genius is knowing how large the business can grow when it is just a seed. So ask yourself, "How many steps am I thinking ahead?"

OUR JOURNEY THUS FAR . . .

DEALMAKER'S COMMANDMENT I: IT IS BETTER TO BE FEARED THAN LOVED.

Being feared is more useful and reliable than being loved.

DEALMAKER'S COMMANDMENT II: POWER LEADS; REASON FOLLOWS.

Power, not reason, drives the outcome of a transaction.

DEALMAKER'S COMMANDMENT III: EVERYONE IS ON THE SAME SIDE . . . THEIR OWN.

Parties are motivated by and can be predicted to behave in accordance with their perceived best self-interest.

DEALMAKER'S COMMANDMENT IV: THINGS ARE PRECISELY AS THEY SEEM.

All manner of irrational and emotional impulses must be shaved away to objectively analyze the battlefield.

DEALMAKER'S COMMANDMENT V: NO PIG WRESTLING.

Combat is honor. Choose your enemies and battles wisely. If combat is thrust upon you, choose to define your enemy and the conditions for victory.

DEALMAKER'S COMMANDMENT VI: TAKE YES FOR YES, MAYBE FOR YES AND NO FOR MAYBE.

Dealmaking is a dance whose basic steps are: offer, counter, close. Conduct the tempo and tune to your advantage.

Now, to conquer time itself!

DEALMAKER'S COMMANDMENT VII: DO IT, DELETE IT, DELEGATE IT.

Hurry up, time is money.

DO IT, DELETE IT, DELEGATE IT

"Dost thou love life? Then do not squander time; for that's the stuff life is made of."

—BENJAMIN FRANKLIN

CREATE YOUR SYSTEM

"I must create a system or be enslaved by another man's."

—William Blake

Time, the invisible jewel. A dealmaker's time is their commodity. That's what you sell. Time spent focusing your intellectual capital on a transaction is what the customer is paying for. By creating a system that maximizes the efficient use of your time, you are able to maximize the value of your labor and expand your circle of influence. New opportunities present themselves. Your power grows.

Being a great dealmaker is about gaining and maintaining control. Control begins with self-control. There is no more fundamental form of self-control than control over how you spend your time. And it all begins with creating a time-management system that works for you.

QUESTION FOR SELF-MASTERY

WHAT IS THE BEST USE OF MY TIME RIGHT NOW?

"Time is at once the most valuable and the most perishable of all our possessions."

—John Randolph

I was reading Bill Clinton's autobiography *My Life,* and I read a passage that changed my life. In the book, he discusses how as a young man he read *How to Get Control of Your Time and Life* by Alan Lakein and how it impacted his ability to effectively manage his time. I had recently started my law firm, and I was completely overwhelmed. I felt like I was drowning, constantly. So much to do. Small things, big things, infrastructure things, things for current clients, trying to get new clients. My health suffered. I gained weight and was not able to take good care of myself. I was underwater, and I needed help. Although, it was out of print, I found a copy on Amazon.

Originally published in 1973, culturally it feels a bit dated, but wow, the meat of it is damn fantastic. Lakein asks you to go through the exercise of asking yourself, "What are my lifetime goals?" Write everything down you can think of. Then refine that list by asking yourself, "How would I like to spend the next three years?" Then refine that further by asking yourself, "If I knew now I would be struck dead by lightning six months from today, how would I live until then?"

You go through the list of lifetime goals and begin to prioritize. The goals most important to you are "A" goals, the less important are "B" goals and the goals of little importance become "C" goals. You further refine those goals. The most important A goal is "A-1." The next is "A-2." The next is "A-3." You then basically chuck the C goals and the B goals as well. You are left with A-1, A-2 and A-3. That is the prism through which you view the world and focus your energy. If you are spending time in a manner that doesn't push you toward your A goals, you are not prioritizing correctly.

I found the exercise to be illuminative. We are surrounded by so much stimulus, so much information, so much input. If we don't choose our priorities, the world thrusts its priorities on us. I started my own business so I could give directions not take them. Previously, I had worked at a large company and was there when they downsized my department. Mass firings. It didn't matter too much to me. I was extremely junior. I was young and had time to figure something else out. But, I witnessed what happened to some of the older executives who were terminated. In a couple of cases, lives were literally ruined. Guys in their early 50s who had done very good work. Loyal company men cast aside through no fault of their own. A couple of my colleagues, better men than me, got knocked down and couldn't get up. I think of it to this day. I'm haunted by it. In part, that's why I started my own company. I wanted to shape my world, not be shaped by it. Control. Dealmakers exert control. Control over themselves, control over their environment. Control is power.

Now, how does one gain that control when you are drowning in a sea of e-mails and calls and choices and obligations? Lakein argues that the way to gain that control is by asking:

"WHAT IS THE BEST USE OF MY TIME RIGHT NOW?"

Look directly into that terrifying maelstrom of chaos. Close your eyes. Breath in. Breathe out. Think about your A goals. How awesome it will be when you accomplish them. Success. Your success. This precise moment, what action can you take that will best propel you closer to achieving an A goal? What is the best use of your time right now? Let the answer to that question shape your actions.

ACTIVITY IS NOT PRODUCTIVITY

"That which is measured improves."
—**Pearson's Law/Karl Pearson**

First facts, then analysis. Take a week and make a journal of how you are spending your time at work. Then give it a cold, hard looksy. What activities are wasting your precious time? What people are wasting your precious time? What part of the day are you most productive? Are you doing your most important activities during that time or wasting your golden time on minutia. How can you tweak your schedule to be more efficient? Make changes, measure again in a few weeks, improve. Rinse and repeat.

In your analysis, be careful not to conflate activity with productivity. It's easy to confuse them. They both take your time. They both take your effort. They both make you feel like something was accomplished. The difference is that at the end of productivity you are closer to achieving your A goals.

DO IT, DELETE IT, DELEGATE IT

"A good plan, violently executed now, is better than a perfect plan next week."
—**General George Patton**

No time to dilly dally, dealmaker. Let's get this party started. You have your A goals chosen. You know what victory looks like. Now, how the hell do you get there? You **"Do It, Delete It, Delegate It."** That's how!

- **Do It**—If an activity is worth doing and I am the only person who can effectively perform the task, I do it.
- **Delete It**—If the activity wastes my time (i.e., doesn't propel me toward my goals, is not necessary for infrastructure/deal management/client development). I delete it. Forget it. Who cares. Never happened.
- **Delegate It**—If an activity is worth doing and I have a colleague, collaborator or automated system that can perform the task effectively, I delegate it.

From a macro perspective the system is simple; it's designed to be simple. However, keep in mind the following nuances when deciding to **Do It, Delete It,** or **Delegate It**:

LESS IS MORE

If you need to meet someone, is it possible to do it over Skype instead of an in-person meeting? If you need to request something from a colleague, can you do it with a quick e-mail instead of a lengthy conversation? Is it really necessary to have the entire staff at those interminable weekly status meetings? In certain circumstances the old school, three martini schmoozing lunch or all-hands-on-deck three-hour meeting in the conference room is appropriate. However, don't waste your time and everyone else's by being old school if it's unwarranted.[1]

REDUCE DISTRACTION/STAY CONNECTED

You have to check your e-mail, but if you check it every 30 seconds, you won't be able to get anything substantive done. You must strike a sustainable balance between staying connected and reducing distraction. This may sound crazy, but try checking your e-mails at work only three times a day. Once when you arrive, a second time after lunch and a third time when you are about to leave the office. You might find that your productivity increases when you spend more time working and less time sending e-mails about working. If you can't strike this balance you are in danger of becoming a reactive pinball bouncing eternally from one e-mail to the next. Also, check your e-mails starting with the most recent. Otherwise, you may be responding to an e-mail request that has already been dealt with.

MINUTIAE/TRIVIAL TASKS

Everyone has mundane but necessary tasks that they must do for their job (i.e., paying bills, reviewing expense reports, etc. . . .). If possible, set a regular time once a week (or better yet, once a month) to do this necessary trivia. Otherwise, these tasks will serve as omnipresent distractions diverting your productivity from more substantive tasks.

THE PARETO PRINCIPAL, AKA THE 80-20 RULE

Way back in 1906, the Italian economist Vilfredo Pareto observed that 20 percent of the pea pods in his garden yielded 80 percent of the peas. He then observed that 80 percent of the land in Italy was owned by 20 percent of the population. Scientists started seeing this ratio all over the

---

1. *The 4-Hour Work Week* by Timothy Ferriss has some great suggestions on the time management front.

place and Boom! **The 80–20 Rule** is born. The big idea is that you likely get 80 percent of your revenue from 20 percent of your accounts. Conversely, it is likely that 20 percent of your accounts (not necessarily the highly profitable ones) take up 80 percent of your time. When allocating your resources, have a focus toward the 20 percent accounts providing 80 percent of the revenue. Additionally, if an account is taking up 80 percent of your time, but only providing 20 percent of your revenue, perhaps it's time to part ways.

BEWARE THE ENTREPRENEURIAL ERROR

I have witnessed a phenomena numerous times that I have dubbed "The Entrepreneurial Error." Certain entrepreneurs are great at starting companies but inhibit their growth by micromanaging their operations. The entrepreneur's passion and attention to detail, which was instrumental for the successful launch of the company, is now becoming a liability. Even though the company is your baby, if you are unable to effectively delegate responsibility, your organization will never develop the systems for large-scale growth. Hire great people and get out of their way.

DON'T TAKE SOMEONE'S MONKEY

People love to walk right in your office, put their monkey on your desk and walk right out your door back to the coffee machine. By "monkey" I mean annoying, time consuming, unprofitable problems. If you are not required to take your coworker's monkey or if you are not being compensated adequately to take your customer's monkey, pick that monkey right up off your desk and put it back on their shoulder where it belongs.[2]

YOUR TEAM

Creating the right team to be able to delegate tasks to is crucial. You have less control over building your team when you work for someone else, but argue for additional subordinates and resources where you can. In addition to your own employees, you need outside experts whose judgment you trust. In my case, there is not enough time in the day to become an expert on estate law, family law and criminal litigation. With experts you can rely on, your power and effectiveness is magnified.

---

2. *The One Minute Manager* by Kenneth H. Blanchard and Spencer Johnson discusses this idea more fully and has some great suggestions for effectively managing employees.

YOUR SUBCONSCIOUS

Try delegating to your subconscious when dealing with a challenging assignment. Read up on the facts before you go to sleep. Maybe your brain will create an interesting solution for you while you are napping. I've found that thinking about a problem before I workout is helpful as well. While I'm listening to my tunes on the treadmill, my brain is having its own workout with my challenge de jour.

NO PING PONG, JUST PROGRESS

"To think is to say no."

—Émile Chartier

As an undergraduate, I had the opportunity to meet a self-made billionaire. I asked him if he could give me any advice. He told me the following:

(1)   Always have control of your capital.
(2)   If you become a success, people will say that you were in the right place at the right time. But, how did you put yourself in the right place? How did you know it was the right time? How did you make the right decision when you were in the right place at the right time?

We have thoroughly discussed the issue of control, but this issue of timing is important as well. When pondering a course of action, there can be a very human tendency to overanalyze, to go back and forth, back and forth, back and forth. This is the right call, no that is the right call, no this is the right call. I refer to this comedic conundrum as "ping pong." It's fun to play ping pong; the problem is that nothing much has been accomplished by the end of the game. It's luxurious to go back and forth and back and forth, therapeutic even. And perhaps you are trying to process a genuinely difficult issue. Maybe your analysis has led you to a dark conclusion that you don't want to accept. But, things are precisely as they seem. Eventually, you must accept the truth. That process can take two weeks or five years. Acceptance is a 100-yard dash or a marathon, your choice.

You must move beyond ping pong to progress, taking the next step that your analysis has led you to. Your choice of action may not be perfect, but as Voltaire wrote, *"The perfect is the enemy of the good."* If every choice must be perfect, we are frozen from making any choices at all.

When you believe you are in the right place and you think it is the right time, make the decision you think is right. Pull the trigger. The alternative?

> *"Of all sad words of tongue or pen, the saddest are these: 'It might have been.'"*
>
> **—John Greenleaf Whittier**

THREE-PEAT

> *"Brevity is the soul of wit."*
>
> **—Shakespeare/*Hamlet Act 2, Scene 2***

In the spirit of time management, I will rapidly explain three tips in the time I would normally explain one. No need to thank me. Buying the book is thanks enough.

1. DEFEAT PROCRASTINATION

> *"Procrastination is the thief of time."*
>
> **—Edward Young**

Parkinson's Law states that *"Work expands to fill the time available for its completion."* This is why, back at school, you would stall until the night before the paper was due and then pull a crazy caffeine-fueled all-nighter, sweatily handing in your report moments before the 9 AM deadline. If you find yourself procrastinating, set deadlines that will compel action. For example, setting a call to discuss a deal with a client will force you to get up to speed to prepare. If frozen by the enormity of a task, use the "Swiss Cheese Method." Poke holes in the task by doing manageable pieces of it to prevent yourself from being overwhelmed.[3]

2. COMPARTMENTALIZATION

> *"My mind is a chest of drawers. When I wish to deal with a subject, I shut all the drawers but the one in which the subject is to be found. When I am wearied, I shut all the drawers and go to sleep."*
>
> **—Napoleon Bonaparte**

---

3. Our old pal Alan Lakein's *How to Get Control of Your Time and Your Life* has some great tactics on this as well.

As a short guy, I can't help but be a big fan of Napoleon. So please forgive me if I seem too effusive. His level of productivity was beyond belief. He rose from complete obscurity to end the horrors of the guillotine-mad French Revolution, completely overhauled the French legal system by drafting the egalitarian Napoleonic Codes, created the Banque de France to get the economy under control, initiated an expansive program of public works to improve French infrastructure and help make Paris the exquisite city it is today, became one of the greatest military leaders in history, and got himself crowned Emperor of France by the Pope. Admittedly, the Battle of Waterloo didn't work out so well, but you get the idea. He accomplished a lot. His secret? Compartmentalization. The human brain does not multitask effectively. Pick your most important problem, open that drawer of information, decide on the best course of action, close that drawer and on to the next one.

3. PLENTY OF TIME

> "Don't say you don't have enough time. You have exactly the same number of hours per day that were given to Helen Keller, Pasteur, Michelangelo, Mother Theresa, Leonardo da Vinci, Thomas Jefferson and Albert Einstein."
>
> **—H. Jackson Brown Jr.**

When you are overwhelmed by your responsibilities and feel there is not enough time in the world to allow you to get done what you need to get done, think of all the amazing people who have gone before you. Their weeks had only seven days. Their days had only 24 hours. Their hours had only 60 minutes. They did great things; so can you.

OUR JOURNEY THUS FAR . . .

DEALMAKER'S COMMANDMENT I: IT IS BETTER TO BE FEARED THAN LOVED.

Being feared is more useful and reliable than being loved.

DEALMAKER'S COMMANDMENT II: POWER LEADS; REASON FOLLOWS.

Power, not reason, drives the outcome of a transaction.

DEALMAKER'S COMMANDMENT III: EVERYONE IS ON THE SAME SIDE . . . THEIR OWN.

Parties are motivated by and can be predicted to behave in accordance with their perceived best self-interest.

DEALMAKER'S COMMANDMENT IV: THINGS ARE PRECISELY AS THEY SEEM.

All manner of irrational and emotional impulses must be shaved away to objectively analyze the battlefield.

DEALMAKER'S COMMANDMENT V: NO PIG WRESTLING.

Combat is honor. Choose your enemies and battles wisely. If combat is thrust upon you, choose to define your enemy and the conditions for victory.

DEALMAKER'S COMMANDMENT VI: TAKE YES FOR YES, MAYBE FOR YES AND NO FOR MAYBE.

Dealmaking is a dance whose basic steps are: offer, counter, close. Conduct the tempo and tune to your advantage.

DEALMAKER'S COMMANDMENT VII: DO IT, DELETE IT, DELEGATE IT.

Time is the dealmaker's commodity. Set goals and create a time-management system to maximize the impact of your labor and resources.

Oh hell, things are going very wrong, very fast . . .

DEALMAKER'S COMMANDMENT VIII: DON'T PANIC, STOP THE BLEEDING, DON'T COMPOUND THE ERROR.

We've got a crisis to manage.

VIII

DON'T PANIC, STOP THE BLEEDING, DON'T COMPOUND THE ERROR

"Everyone has a plan until they get punched in the face."

—MIKE TYSON

CHAPTER OUTLINE

Training Replaces Instinct

Don't Panic, Stop the Bleeding, Don't Compound the Error

Solve the Problem Now

What Went Wrong?

Lay Blame without Laying Waste

Improve the Algorithm

TRAINING REPLACES INSTINCT

"The more you sweat in training, the less you bleed in combat."
—**Navy SEALs**

In situations of tremendous stress and danger, humans will resort to instinct or training. Rigorous military training is designed so that soldiers will disregard powerful instincts for self-preservation that ironically would get them killed in combat. That gut reaction to run like hell is beat out of them in boot camp and replaced with trained responses. They learn to adhere to military protocol, to follow orders. Now, when the soldier is in a life-or-death situation, they have a methodology to survive, to complete their mission.

"Don't Panic, Stop the Bleeding, Don't Compound the Error" is the methodology I have developed to replace my instincts when I have made a mistake with consequences. It has saved my butt many times and can save yours as well. When all hell breaks loose, impulsively running away, being frozen with fear or lashing out at the first target you see will likely just make the situation worse. You need training, a methodology ingrained in that beautiful noggin that just got whacked with a sledgehammer.

DON'T PANIC, STOP THE BLEEDING, DON'T COMPOUND THE ERROR

"Nothing gives a person so much advantage over another as to remain always cool and unruffled under all circumstances."
—**Thomas Jefferson**

You just took a haymaker to the dome. Your stomach is in your mouth. The world is fuzzy. Chest tightens. It went wrong, south, sideways. You just got downsized. The deal is imploding. Your wife just left. Mom found the *Playboys*. The market tanked. You got caught. Things got real, real quick. What the hell do you do now?

- **Don't Panic**—Breathe in. Breathe out. It's OK. It's OK. It's all right. I'm here. I'm going to figure this out. It's cool. I got this. Don't panic. There is a solution. I'm going to figure out a solution. I will make this better. Just breathe. Be calm. Don't panic.

- **Stop the Bleeding**—What have I done that is causing damage? Stop doing that.
- **Don't Compound the Error**—Don't act impulsively to attempt to fix the situation. You need to take a moment. You need a minute to think, to analyze. Your gut reaction to the fear you are experiencing is not conducive to reason. At this critical juncture, if you act impulsively you may very well make the situation worse. The absolute last thing you want to do is compound the damage from the initial error by making a subsequent error.

If you took a big hit in the stock market, don't borrow money on margin to buy more shares to try to make up for the hit to your portfolio. It will likely compound your economic loses.

If you didn't think the opposing side was going to walk, don't impulsively chase them down and beg them to come back to the negotiating table. It will compound your loss of face in front of your side and destroy any potential leverage with the opposing side if they do come back.

If you "break the seal" on your low-carb diet by eating some cake, don't beat yourself up and self-flagellate by eating up the rest of the bakery. It will compound your chunkiness.

"Don't Panic, Stop the Bleeding, Don't Compound the Error" is not about making things better, it is about stopping things from getting worse. Trying to stop everything from going wrong while simultaneously trying to make everything go right is likely an overly complex move. It's too clever by half. Dollars to donuts it will blow up in your face. Take things one crucial step at a time. First, stop the damage. Hopefully this buys you some time to objectively assess the situation and discover a solution based on reason, not panic. It's the Hippocratic oath for dealmakers, "First, deal no harm."

SOLVE THE PROBLEM NOW

"When skating on thin ice our safety is in our speed."
—Ralph Waldo Emerson

Now that the bleeding has stopped (or hopefully slowed) and you have not made matters worse, it's time to fix the problem. Move deliberately, but expeditiously. Don't worry about placing blame. Don't worry about the big picture. Don't raise your hands to the heavens shouting "Why?!?! Why?!?! What does it all mean?" Marshal your resources, wrangle your team and fix the problem. If you can't fix the problem, take evasive action to limit the damage. There will be plenty of time for macro-postmortem analysis later. Fixing the problem is about the micro, having laser-like focus on a discrete issue. Also, remember Benjamin Disraeli's advice *"Never complain and never explain."* If you made a mistake, no one wants to hear why you made it or how difficult things are. That's not their problem nor should it be. It makes you seem like an unreliable clown. You were engaged to do a job, so complete the job. Just shut up and fix the problem.

WHAT WENT WRONG?

"To avoid criticism, say nothing, do nothing, be nothing."
—Aristotle

Once the emergency has been dealt with, it's time for the postmortem. What went wrong? Let's bring in the usual suspects:

INSUFFICIENT CLIENT COMMUNICATION

When you are not a principal to a transaction but representing a client, remember the deal is the client's, not yours. You are the tip of the spear, fighting for their interests, but don't confuse that with the deal actually being yours. Your client needs to be fully informed on the current situation. Don't let your client be surprised. It's your job to make sure that they are never surprised. Additionally, clients need to be pulling the trigger on key decisions. If you feel there is danger up ahead, inform them of the risks and rewards and let them call the shots. It's their deal, you are just the avatar.

NO EXIT STRATEGY

There's a marvelous Spanish proverb: *"I don't want the cheese, I just want to get out of the trap."* At the beginning of a deal, the parties are smiling, laughing and slapping each other on the back at overpriced steak dinners. *"Everything is going to be awesome. We are going to make so much damn money!"* That enthusiasm has its place and hopefully everything works out great. But, what if it doesn't? What if creatively or economically the parties don't see eye to eye? What if the parties are never able to build the trust necessary for a successful business partnership? What if the product they are selling never catches on, and each side of the deal wants to take their ball and bounce?

Did you build an escape hatch into your transaction? Is there a clean way to get out if things have gone wrong? Don't let your deal be the Titanic. Make sure there are plenty of life boats in case this bad boy hits an iceberg.

THE COVER UP

Regarding Watergate, Richard Nixon famously said, *"What really hurts is if you try to cover it up."* Tricky Dick was right. The initial mistake may be so egregious that attempting to cover it up is the only thing that prevents you from the electric chair, but most of the time it is not. Be proactive, get ahead of the scandal and admit the mistake. By taking the lead you are controlling the release of information and can spin it to your advantage if possible. People can be more forgiving than you expect. Ironically, if you admit a mistake, people are often more willing to trust you. They know that if there is a problem, you will level with them.

Conversely, if you get nailed attempting to cover something up, you are toast. People understand that mistakes are made in the heat of battle or at a drunken industry convention, but a cover up? Cover ups don't occur after a three martini dinner. Cover ups are cooked up at noon over coffee. Cover ups are well thought out, intentional attempts to trick people. That makes people think that you think they are stupid. People don't like that. If you are caught trying to execute the cover up, the audience you are trying to deceive will be angry. Perhaps angry enough to eject you from the presidency.

QUESTION FOR SELF-MASTERY

AT THE TIME, WAS MY DECISION *COMPLETELY* UNREASONABLE?

"There can be no real freedom without the freedom to fail."
—**Eric Hoffer**

When I used to make a mistake I would be really brutal on myself. It was weird actually. I would play the mistake over and over and over in my mind like some terrible horror movie on repeat. When the error was going to be made, I would yell at the screen in my mind. "Jeff, don't do it! Don't go into the barn! Whatever you do, don't go into the barn! The killer's in the barn!" But, it was too late; the mistake had already been made. I was just watching the movie. I would inevitably go into the barn, and things would deteriorate from there. Self-loathing, shame, despair. "Why the hell did I do that?"

I think some of it might stem from having been a child actor. When I was a kid and I didn't get the hot dog commercial I auditioned for, bills might not get paid. Things would be bad, and it was my fault. Yes, that's messed up on a lot of levels, but the embarrassment and cost of failure stuck with me. As an adult, I realized that this incessant self-recrimination was not helpful. It was not noble; it was masochism.

"Sadness is a vice."

—Gustave Flaubert

I had to find a way to stop these dumb movies from playing in my head. After watching my mistake movie once, there was nothing more to get out of it. I know how it turns out. Why perseverate on the failure? What is the use in that?

So, I developed a methodology to allow me to deal with my failures. Be brutally honest, but not brutally callous. First apply brutal (i.e., honest) criticism of your mistake. I did X, I should have done Y. That sucks, fine. Next time I'm in that situation I will do Y, not X.

But, then when the movie of my failure would begin to repeat in my mind, I would stop the film projector, turn on the lights and ask a very precise question:

"At the time, was my decision completely *unreasonable?"*

The choice that I made, without the benefit of 20/20 hindsight, at the time I made it, was it *completely* unreasonable? Was there absolutely zero basis in reason for making the decision I did? Invariably, the answer is "No, my decision was not *completely* unreasonable." There was some kernel of reason for making the choice I made. It may have been a dumb reason or desire or hope; it may not have been completely reasonable, but it was certainly not *completely* unreasonable either. It was likely a very human decision, and humans are not Gods. Humans make mistakes. It's part of the gig. Answering this Question for Self-Mastery has enabled me to be a kind parent to myself, to forgive myself and move forward from my past mistakes. The present is a present; let's focus our energy there.

LAY BLAME WITHOUT LAYING WASTE

"The man who makes no mistakes usually does not make anything."
—William Conner Magee

You have analyzed factually what went wrong with the disaster de jour. Then, you have asked, "At the time, was my decision *completely* unreasonable?" to turn the analysis inward. The next step is to look at the people around you. This should not be an exercise in shirking personal responsibility or throwing others under the bus to protect yourself. This is not about constructing a "narrative of blame" so that the powerful can scapegoat the less powerful to ensure that the master is never wrong.

"Laying blame without laying waste" is about taking an honest and objective look at the players around you. How did your team members behave during the conflagration? Who was straight with you? Who tried to cover things up? Who rose to the challenge? Who hid? The way a person behaves during these high-pressure situations, reveals their character. If you can depend on someone in a foxhole, that is something. Perhaps, that person should be given more power in your organization. Conversely, if your collaborator waved the white flag of surrender before the first shot was fired, file that little chestnut away in your mind for future use as well. Discovering who can be depended on when the chips are down is a nice byproduct of going through hell together.

"My great concern is not whether you have failed, but whether you are content with your failure."

—Abraham Lincoln

Having the power of judgment over others is a tricky tightrope to walk. On one hand, your subordinates and collaborators are human. If people try anything challenging, mistakes are likely to be made. On the other hand, if they are careless or incompetent, your cause will suffer. Maybe you have to cut some stragglers loose? Bad behavior does require consequences and a dealmaker's margin for error is slim, very slim. My key metrics for judging those around me are competence and desire. Both components are necessary. The difference being that competence can be taught, desire cannot. You can't make them want it.

IMPROVE THE ALGORITHM

"You can never make the same mistake twice because the second time you make it, it's not a mistake, it's a choice."

—Steven Denn

Henry Ford is arguably the greatest industrialist of the twentieth century. Anti-Semitic rantings aside, he was a genius who revolutionized mass production and transformed the very landscape of America. His masterpiece was the Model T, the first car produced economically enough for working-class people to afford. The Model T first rolled off the assembly line in 1908. By 1918, 50 percent of all cars in the United States were Model Ts. Standardization was key to Ford's philosophy.

"Any customer can have a car painted any color he wants so long as it is black."

—Henry Ford

To say that Ford was resistant to change was putting it lightly. While automotive technology moved forward and tastes changed, he refused to update his design. Eventually, Ford Motors had lost so much market share that even Henry Ford agreed it was time to shake things up. The last Model T rolled off the assembly line in 1927. Could you imagine a car manufacturer not updating their model for 19 years? It's a testament to the brilliance of the original design, but it's also a cautionary tale about the dangers of being resistant to change.

Let's compare that to Silicon Valley's ethos. The software on your mobile device will likely be automatically updated every 19 days, not 19 years. Finding the bug and fixing the bug is not shameful; it's laudable. Consistent, incremental improvement is the way of the world.

Of course, Charles Darwin had figured this one out a while ago, and nature had been doing it for a few eons before that. Evolution surrounds us and must be a part of our dealmaking process. "Crisis is opportunity" because it provides a delicious opportunity to evolve. Dealmakers are not "one and done." We negotiate hundreds of deals, thousands of deals. We are deal engineers. We must learn from our mistakes, where the contract has failed, and fix the bug for version 2.0 and 2.1 and 2.2. It's OK to stumble on occasion; it means you are challenging yourself. No shame in that. But there is shame in not being willing to admit your mistakes and improve the algorithm. Resist evolution and you resist the very fabric of the universe itself.

INTERNAL COMMUNICATION

"A gossip is one who talks to you about others; a bore is one who talks to you about himself; and a brilliant conversationalist is one who talks to you about yourself."

—Lisa Kirk

Given that miscommunication with clients or collaborators is such a prodigious cause of snafus, let's take a look at some tips on improving internal communication.

LISTEN

When I would go on dates, often I would be super nervous and break the inevitable uncomfortable silences with whatever dumb stuff came into my head. *"Hey, uh . . . clowns are pretty scary don't you think? Damn, I hate clowns."* This turned out to be an ineffective methodology, so I created a different one. It was simple, but a great improvement. I shifted my focus from speaking to listening. If there was an awkward silence, I would ask a polite question and listen. People love when you listen to their stories. People hunger to be listened to. It shows them that you care about their thoughts and about them as people. It's also fun, once you get good at it. If you love learning, you should love listening. If you want to be a great communicator with clients, collaborators and with dates for that matter, be a great listener above all. That skill is more rare than you would imagine.

QUIET IS KEPT

In *The Godfather*, Sonny Corleone opened up his big mouth and contradicted his father, Don Vito Corleone, at their meeting with Sollozzo the Turk. From Sonny's offhanded remark, the Turk saw potential dissension in the Corleone Family, started a mob war and put Don Vito in the hospital after a failed assassination attempt. Don Vito's angry admonition to Sonny still holds: *"Never tell anyone outside the Family what you are thinking again!"*

As a lawyer, I have a specific and sacred duty of confidentiality with my clients. Clients need to know that they can be completely open and honest with me without fear of the information getting out. I need complete candor with a client to be able to give them the best possible advice. This is why you should never lie to your doctor and never lie to your lawyer. When people learn that they can trust you to keep your mouth shut, you become privy to more information. More information leads to better advice leads to better choices. Quiet is kept.

OVERLAPPING INTERESTS

Perhaps the best way to facilitate effective internal communication is to structure the economic arrangement so that everyone's incentives are aligned. If the partners of a venture have relatively equal amounts of power and the profits are fairly distributed with transparent accounting, then everyone has overlapping interests. What's in my best interest is also in yours. There is no need for subterfuge when everyone is on the same side of the table and information is not hidden. It's not often that the stars align to allow this to happen, but when it does things can feel downright collegial. As Walter Sickert said: "*Nothing knits man to man like the frequent passing, from hand to hand, of cash.*"

OUR JOURNEY THUS FAR . . .

DEALMAKER'S COMMANDMENT I: IT IS BETTER TO BE FEARED THAN LOVED.

Being feared is more useful and reliable than being loved.

DEALMAKER'S COMMANDMENT II: POWER LEADS; REASON FOLLOWS.

Power, not reason, drives the outcome of a transaction.

DEALMAKER'S COMMANDMENT III: EVERYONE IS ON THE SAME SIDE . . . THEIR OWN.

Parties are motivated by and can be predicted to behave in accordance with their perceived best self-interest.

DEALMAKER'S COMMANDMENT IV: THINGS ARE PRECISELY AS THEY SEEM.

All manner of irrational and emotional impulses must be shaved away to objectively analyze the battlefield.

DEALMAKER'S COMMANDMENT V: NO PIG WRESTLING.

Combat is honor. Choose your enemies and battles wisely. If combat is thrust upon you, choose to define your enemy and the conditions for victory.

DEALMAKER'S COMMANDMENT VI: TAKE YES FOR YES, MAYBE FOR YES AND NO FOR MAYBE.

Dealmaking is a dance whose basic steps are: offer, counter, close. Conduct the tempo and tune to your advantage.

DEALMAKER'S COMMANDMENT VII: DO IT, DELETE IT, DELEGATE IT.

Time is the dealmaker's commodity. Set goals and create a time-management system to maximize the impact of your labor and resources.

DEALMAKER'S COMMANDMENT VIII: DON'T PANIC, STOP THE BLEEDING, DON'T COMPOUND THE ERROR.

Train yourself to calmly and effectively handle emergencies. Then, fix the problem, analyze the error and improve the algorithm.

What does it all mean anyways? Where do we belong in this crazy world?

DEALMAKER'S COMMANDMENT IX: BE A DEALMAKER, NOT A DEAL BREAKER

That will help us figure it out.

BE A DEALMAKER, NOT A DEAL BREAKER

"A wise man will make more opportunities than he finds."

—SIR FRANCIS BACON

CHAPTER OUTLINE

Know Your Role

What a Dealmaker Is

What a Dealmaker Ain't

Pros Get Paid

Pros Play Hurt

The Art of Good Business

KNOW YOUR ROLE

"Acting is a masochistic form of exhibitionism. It is not quite the occupation of an adult."

—Sir Laurence Olivier

Sometimes being a dealmaker feels like a masochistic form of exhibitionism as well. Like actors, dealmakers play a part. Sometimes we're the lead. Sometimes we're a supporting player.

Can you adapt your style and govern your instincts based upon the role you are playing? If so, you will avoid being typecast and will have more opportunities available to you. **Dealmaker's Commandment IX: Be a Dealmaker, Not a Deal Breaker** is about having awareness of our place in the deal and being mindful of our relationship with the other parties. And then there's that little matter of what we are getting out of all this. How are we being compensated, and what is our place in the Motivation Mosaic we discussed in Chapter 3?

The first step toward knowing your role as a dealmaker in a particular transaction is to understand if you are a **Representative, Partner or Principal:**

- **Representative**—A representative acts to further the interests of their client. In an entertainment context representatives include: lawyers, agents, managers, publicists and business managers. It is your role and duty to pursue and protect your client's welfare. The word Esquire (Esq) has a common etymological origin with the word 'Squire'. Lawyers are squires in service of our knight, the client.
- **Partner**—In a partnership or joint venture, you act to further the collective interests of the group. It's tricky in that you have to protect your interests from your collaborators while simultaneously advocating the interests of your collaborators. Partnership is like marriage, a great institution. But, who wants to live in an institution? The key idea for a dealmaker as partner is to strike the right balance between your interests and the interests of the partnership.
- **Principal**—This is where the real cheddar is! The boss, big baller, shot caller, owner, capitalist, titan of industry. When you are both dealmaker and principal, you get to feel the sweet exhilaration of being an unmitigated, unfiltered greedy bastard. You are overtly acting in furtherance of you own interests. Your power is plenary. But with great power comes great responsibility. You receive the

lion's share of the reward if things work out and the lion's share of the risk if it doesn't.

As we learned in **Dealmaker's Commandment III**, ultimately everyone acts in furtherance of their own perceived best self-interests. However, we need to know if we are a Representative, Partner or Principal to ascertain precisely where those interests lie.

WHAT A DEALMAKER IS

"A.B.C. A-Always, B-Be, C-Closing. Always be closing, always be closing."

—**Blake/***Glengarry Glen Ross*

A.B.C. Always be closing. Always be closing. Always be closing. Chant it, whisper it, holler it to the heavens. Always Be Closing is the dealmaker's mantra. Regardless of the type of dealmaker you choose to become, at the end of the day, dealmakers make deals. Ultimately reaching a mutually agreed upon transaction gets everyone paid. No deal, no dough. Like anything, there are exceptions that prove the rule. On occasion, you have to destroy your opposition instead of closing a deal to make a point. Sometimes it can be advantageous to intentionally keep a deal open. But, both tactics are used to create an atmosphere in the marketplace that facilitates more moolah moving forward.

Every situation has its own needs, but with closing at the forefront of your mind, here are some things that a dealmakers is:

A HUB OF KNOWLEDGE AND RELATIONSHIPS

Dealmakers are unique in that we work on a large volume of diverse transactions. Thus we become extremely knowledgeable about industry trends and practices in the marketplace. This puts us in a great position to advise our clients and collaborators of the most advantageous way to price and structure deals. Additionally, we are working with a variety of people on each transaction, both on our side and the opposing side. Perhaps, it is advantageous to bring in my ally from a previous transaction on a new transaction. Conversely, if I am negotiating against someone now that I have negotiated against previously, I know their go-to moves and tendencies. This knowledge adds strength to my team's position.

THE FOX AND THE LION

Machiavelli puts forth this beautiful idea in *The Prince* that in order to be a successful leader *"it is necessary to be a fox to discover the snares and a lion to terrify the wolves."* A successful dealmaker must be a fox and a lion as well. Foxes are clever and paranoid, sniffing around high and low for danger. Anyone can be paranoid recreationally, but I get to do it for a living. Everyone is actively trying to trick, trap and troll you and your client. My paranoia helps me discover and neutralize contractual snares that would otherwise damage my team. It is also necessary to be ferocious like a lion. People have to be afraid of you. The Power Punishment Paradigm is brought to bear. If you have a mechanism to inflict punishment, you will use it. The other side knows this. They keep their distance.

A DIPLOMAT

When the opposing sides are evenly matched, the ability to be diplomatic is crucial. Two parties of equal strength going to war is often a pointless exercise in mutual destruction. Bruising round after bruising round, and the parties will likely fight to a draw. Instead, diplomatically broker a mutually beneficial treaty. Save your ammo for a more vulnerable and valuable target.

A BODYGUARD

When I'm acting as a client's bodyguard, I try to be a mix between Clint Eastwood and Boba Fett. I get really quiet, really serious and scrunch my eyes like I'm getting ready to draw my pistol at a gunfight. Sometimes, I'll attend a meeting with my client, allied reps and the opposing side and say almost nothing. I'm not there to yap. I'm there as a warning. Be cool or my guys let me off the leash. And who needs that?

To that end, I'm always cc'd on accounting statements and profit participation reports for deals I have closed. The opposing side needs to know that I am constantly monitoring things so nobody gets cute with the books.

AN OPPORTUNIST

One of the most valuable things dealmakers do is to spot opportunities for themselves and their allies. Given the volume of marketplace information we are privy to, being entrepreneurial is a natural extension of transactional representation. You see the opportunity, identify the necessary pieces for the venture, bring them together, set the economic structure and build something. With a little luck, maybe you build something great.

WHAT A DEALMAKER AIN'T

"Being powerful is like being a lady. If you have to tell people you are, you aren't."
—**Margaret Thatcher**

Part of knowing your role is knowing when to shut up. You exist to close deals, not to show everyone in the room how smart you are, how loud you can yell and how cool your car is. You serve the deal, the client, the collective interests of your side. Don't be a diva. No one is there to bask in your glory or soak up your good looks and wit. Blowhards get blown up. With that in mind, here are some things that a dealmaker ain't:

A BARRISTER

In England lawyers are actually divided into two distinct professions. Solicitors draft and negotiate contracts. Barristers are litigators who get to wear those awesome wigs and argue at the bar in front of the judge who also gets to wear an awesome wig. As a bald guy, it would be a great perk to get to wear one of those wigs, but alas, we are not barristers. We are solicitors. We want to make deals, not court appearances. It's fine to use litigation as a threat and in certain cases it is completely appropriate to pursue civil action. However, for a dealmaker that must be the exception. You exist to create a great deal, not to create a great lawsuit.

A PREACHER

Reportedly, Maya Angelou's favorite quote was a real gem from the ancient Roman poet Terence: *"I am human being; nothing human can be alien to me."* As a dealmaker you have a front row, center seat to the great and terrible circus of humanity. You're going to see a lot of interesting stuff, up close and personal: duplicity, greed, lust and anger to start. Take a deep breath . . . and accept it. All that ugliness is just part of the human condition. Which makes it a part of me, you and everyone. We all have our vices, our weaknesses. We are not here to judge or moralize or show everyone right from wrong. There are other social institutions to serve that function. We are here to make a deal. So keep your eyes open, mouth shut and save the sermon for Sunday school.

BLOOD THIRSTY

Part of our job is hurting people. At its essence, that's what fighting is. You hurt the other side. They no longer want to be hurt. Then they give you what you want so you will stop pummeling them. Combat is frightening and exhilarating and challenging and horrific all at once. But you engage in combat to achieve a goal. You do not engage in combat because it's fun to punch someone in the throat. This is not sport. You are dealing with people's livelihoods and the well-being of their families, both on your side and the opposing side. We strike like a professional boxer strikes, in order to win the fight and the fat prize purse that comes with it. We are not barbarians. We are not animals. We are thirsty for victory, not blood.

A MAGICIAN

Trust me, there are plenty of times I wish I could pull a David Copperfield and make my enemies disappear. Even the greatest dealmaker cannot wave a wand and turn a terrible deal into a gleaming diamond. Per our GAT-NALYSIS, we are limited by our gun (the client's inherent leverage) and our ammo (the client's will to fight). The final results we achieve are a function of our ability and the tools we are working with. We can't sculpt the statue of David without a really big block of marble.

INDISPENSABLE

Charles de Gaulle said, *"The graveyards are full of indispensable men."* Remember, we are not irreplaceable. No one is. Don't get cocky. Don't get too full of yourself. When serving as a rep, you wield your client's power, but you are not the source of your client's power. It's easy to confuse that. Don't outshine the master. Play your part. Know your role.

PROS GET PAID

"A retainer is how the client knows he has a lawyer and the lawyer knows he has a client."

—Abraham Lincoln

I was filming a scene once back when I was a kid actor. Half-jokingly, I asked my director "What's my motivation?" The director paused for a moment, looked at me and replied . . ."Money." It was said in jest of course. But every joke is a confession. The fundamental distinction between an amateur and a professional is that a professional gets paid. If you're doing something and not making money for doing it, it's not a job; it's a hobby. We've spent a lot of time discussing what dealmakers do and how they should do it, but we have not discussed how they get compensated for doing it. This subject is close to my heart. When determining your fee structure, here are some things to keep in mind:

SET YOUR FEE PRIOR TO COMMENCING WORK

Everyone loves free stuff. Free, free, free! Just make sure your valuable services are not part of that free stuff that everyone is loving. If you are not careful, it's easy to drift into representing someone before your fee is set. You answer a question, then another set of questions, then a meeting, then a Skype conference. You are in business. Too late to bail. After an initial consultation, it is important to set how you will be paid with your client or business partner as the case may be. If your collaborator or client cannot or will not compensate you appropriately, better to know at the beginning. You're a dealmaker. Time is your commodity. Waste it at your peril.

GET A SIGNED FEE AGREEMENT PRIOR TO COMMENCING WORK

Once your fee is agreed to, have a brief signed agreement codifying the arrangement. People have a funny habit of forgetting their obligations if they are not in writing. If your client or collaborator dings you on your remuneration, they now may face a lawsuit for breach of the written agreement. Better to be feared than loved, right?

ALIGN YOUR FEE STRUCTURE WITH YOUR CLIENT'S INTERESTS

The best possible fee structure is one that puts you on the same side of the table as your client. For example, if I am a doing a deal for a director, I receive a percentage of the money the director receives from the contract I negotiate. I am incentivized to get the director as much money as possible, because that means more money for little ol' me. If a percentage is not appropriate, then I prefer a flat fee instead of charging the client hourly. A flat fee creates clarity, and there is no incentive to drag out the negotiation if it doesn't make sense. Usually the client wants to close their deal expeditiously as does their rep. Contrast this with hourly billing, which incentivizes the rep to drag things out. Anyone who has received those fantastic hourly billing statements from a drawn-out litigation knows what I mean. Ughhhhhhh . . .

COMPETE ON QUALITY, NOT PRICE

Don't be the cheapest; be the best. Depending on your industry, there will be a market range for services provided. You want be paid toward the higher end of that spectrum. People will pay for superior quality. Do great work to justify great compensation.

"A man who is his own lawyer has a fool for a client," so the legal maxim goes. Setting your compensation is difficult for precisely that reason. Being your own advocate is weird. It feels distasteful and braggadocios to argue how valuable you are. It is uncomfortable, but it is also necessary. If you don't fight for your own economic interests, who will? The good news is that it gets easier as time goes on. As your reputation and body of work grows, the precedent for how your fees are set grows as well. Physician, heal thyself, and dealmaker, deal thyself!

PROS PLAY HURT

"Feelings are luxuries. Actions are necessities."

—Me

I love those old NFL films where they interview players from back in the day. When football helmets had one slim crossbar in the front and just about everything was legal. If you ever watch some of those old games from the late 50s and early 60s, it's quite insane. Horse-collar tackles, clothesline tackles, the head slap, hitting below the knees: all legal. And during that brutal era of the NFL, the most brutal division was the "NFC Central" comprising the Chicago Bears, Detroit Lions, Green Bay Packers and Minnesota Vikings. It was nicknamed the "Black and Blue Division" because those teams were bitter rivals and would just beat the hell out of each other week after week. I watched an interview with the great defensive lineman Alex Karras, who played for the Lions during that period. The interviewer asked what it meant to him to be a professional athlete. Karras took a beat to think about the question then said that anyone can play healthy. It's easy to play football healthy. Amateurs can play healthy. But, professionals can play hurt.

"You might say, pain is my co-pilot."

—Alex Karras

Karras' response stuck with me. He was right. Professionals play at the highest level even through excruciating pain. I can't imagine the pain he had to endure en route to his four trips to the Pro Bowl, but by the look in his eyes when he answered that question, it must have been tremendous. The damage received. The damage inflicted. Pros play hurt. Yes, they do.

Fortunately, dealmakers are unlikely to get clotheslined at Soldier Field on a chilly Chicago Sunday. But you will take damage. Friends become "frenemies" become mortal enemies. Having the wind knocked out of you after being slugged in the gut by the unforeseen double cross. Getting stabbed in the back by your "ally," not to mention the overt horrors inflicted by your opposition. Assaulting your character. Attacking your intellect. Attempting to impugn your reputation. Competitors trying to steal your business, destroy your livelihood, eat your lunch. You will take damage. You will feel fear, anger, pain and, worst of all, disappointment.

The beauty of feelings is that you can feel however you want. That's your freedom. That's your right. Feelings are luxuries. Luxuriate in your anger. Take a bubble bath in your disappointment. Go to a dimly lit coffee shop and journal about your fears to your caffeinated heart's content. Sulk to your favorite dive bar and drink the pain into oblivion. Whatever floats your boat.

Actions, however, are necessities. Being in pain does not relieve you of your obligation to make the correct decision. You need to perform at the highest level regardless of how you feel. You need to take the right course of action, rain or shine. The margin for error is remarkably slim. The stakes are too high and competition too fierce. To be an all-pro dealmaker, you have to bring your "A" game, even when you're hurt. Especially when you're hurt, actually. If the game is getting that ferocious, that means the stakes are probably worth fighting for.

THE ART OF GOOD BUSINESS

"Always remember, the art of good business is being a good middle man."
—Eddie Temple/*Layer Cake*

Ultimately, a great dealmaker is a great middle man. That may not sound glamorous, but it is accurate. Sometimes we are diplomats. Sometimes we are advocates. Sometimes we are bodyguards. Sometimes we spot the opportunity and bring the pieces together. But, in all cases, we are in the middle: the middle of the fight, the middle of the deal, the middle of the action. Is it glamorous? Occasionally. Is it profitable? Consistently.

SHOW UP

"Eighty percent of success is showing up."

—Woody Allen

Whatever your industry, there are invariably a number of events that you will be invited to. This seems fun at first, but after your hundredth schmoozy cocktail party, the thought of attending another one after a long day at work probably makes you want to jump off a bridge. I always get anxious when I am preparing to attend a business conference, film festival or industry-related event. I like being in control of my time and having a plan of action. With industry events, you can't really control what happens. Maybe you will have an uncomfortable run-in with your nemesis de jour? Maybe parking will be a big mess? Maybe you will get trapped by some boring blowhard giving a 30 minute monologue about how amazing their business is going? That's the thing with industry events, you don't know what will happen if you show up. But you do know what will happen if you don't show up. Nothing.

Attending the shindig injects you into the stream of commerce and that's where you need to be. You can feel anxious and exhausted, but you still must be on stage when the curtain rises. Many great performers suffer from stage fright. It's almost a proverb that the better the performer is, the more nervous they get before the show. Once the play begins, you will remember your lines, hit your marks and the audience of partygoers will adore you. Maybe you will make a great new connection? Maybe you will discover a delicious nugget of gossip that helps you on your current venture? A lot might happen if you show up, but nothing will happen if you don't. That's for certain.

QUESTION FOR SELF-MASTERY

WHAT DO I REALLY WANT?

"I cannot give you the formula for success, but I can give you the formula for failure—which is: Try to please everybody."
—**Herbert Bayard Swope**

Ask yourself, "What do I really want?" Not, what your family wants or your church wants or your boss wants, what do you want? What do you really want?

This Question for Self-Mastery is deceptively simple but can be quite difficult to answer. We are trained from an early age to figure out what others want. We ascertain someone's expectations then meet or exceed them. That's how you get ahead, right? When you are a kid, you behave how everyone wants you to behave at dinner, then you get a treat. In school, you give the teachers what they want and get good grades. You give the people who make the college aptitude exam what they want and get in to a good university. You give your professors what they want and get into a good graduate school. You give your grad school professors what they want and get a good job. You give your bosses what they want and . . . what happens then?

In our fluid marketplace, the odds of working at one place your entire career are remote. Every day, talented, hard-working people are fired from their jobs for macroeconomic reasons having nothing to do with their performance. The linear path begins to curve. There are no more teachers to please. You are faced with unlimited choices, responsibilities and risks. In this tumultuous sea of opportunity, your North Star is knowing what you want, how you feel and what you think. This self-knowledge enables you to set goals that are exciting, fulfilling and emblematic of you as a person.

"Your time is limited, so don't waste it living someone else's life."
—**Steve Jobs**

As dealmakers we have many roles to play. Each role comes with important obligations to our clients and collaborators and constituents. We must be able to meet our responsibilities to others while still pursuing our own path. Otherwise, when finally we reach our goals we will discover they were actually someone else's. It's impossible to achieve your goals if they're not *your* goals.

OUR JOURNEY THUS FAR . . .

DEALMAKER'S COMMANDMENT I: IT IS BETTER TO BE FEARED THAN LOVED.

Being feared is more useful and reliable than being loved.

DEALMAKER'S COMMANDMENT II: POWER LEADS; REASON FOLLOWS.

Power, not reason, drives the outcome of a transaction.

DEALMAKER'S COMMANDMENT III: EVERYONE IS ON THE SAME SIDE . . . THEIR OWN.

Parties are motivated by and can be predicted to behave in accordance with their perceived best self-interest.

DEALMAKER'S COMMANDMENT IV: THINGS ARE PRECISELY AS THEY SEEM.

All manner of irrational and emotional impulses must be shaved away to objectively analyze the battlefield.

DEALMAKER'S COMMANDMENT V: NO PIG WRESTLING.

Combat is honor. Choose your enemies and battles wisely. If combat is thrust upon you, choose to define your enemy and the conditions for victory.

DEALMAKER'S COMMANDMENT VI: TAKE YES FOR YES, MAYBE FOR YES AND NO FOR MAYBE.

Dealmaking is a dance whose basic steps are: offer, counter, close. Conduct the tempo and tune to your advantage.

DEALMAKER'S COMMANDMENT VII: DO IT, DELETE IT, DELEGATE IT.

Time is the dealmaker's commodity. Set goals and create a time-management system to maximize the impact of your labor and resources.

DEALMAKER'S COMMANDMENT VIII: DON'T PANIC, STOP THE BLEEDING, DON'T COMPOUND THE ERROR.

Train yourself to calmly and effectively handle emergencies. Then, fix the problem, analyze the error and improve the algorithm.

DEALMAKER'S COMMANDMENT IX: BE A DEALMAKER, NOT A DEAL BREAKER

Dealmakers make deals. Know your role, get paid and remember your ABCs. Always be closing.

Dealmaking can be dark business. How does one keep from going mad?

DEALMAKER'S COMMANDMENT X: HEED NIETZSCHE'S WARNING.

That's how.

HEED NIETZSCHE'S WARNING

"Whoever fights monsters should beware that he, himself,

does not become a monster."

—FRIEDRICH NIETZSCHE

CHAPTER OUTLINE

The Fog of War

The Cost to Be the Boss

Forbearance

Shelter From the Storm

THE FOG OF WAR

"The dominant feeling of the battlefield is loneliness"
—Field Marshal William Slim

Being a dealmaker is a life of constant combat. Like any form of prolonged stress, it changes you. Sometime you are fighting bad people. Bad people do bad things. You have to do bad things in return. Or perhaps you do bad things preemptively to block the bad things you anticipate they will do. Things get fuzzy. Who was the bad guy again? You remember that you are fighting for something noble: to further your client's interests. And your client is the good guy, right? Wait, am I David or Goliath in this one? OK, I'm David on this one and my opponent is a big, mean SOB. I can just about reach his kneecap, which fortunately for me is unarmored. If I hit him in the knee hard enough, it going to hurt him or at least distract him long enough to buy me some time. CRACK! Oh, that did hurt him. Weak spot. Hit it again. Harder. Hit it again. He's down. Hit it again. Harder. Hit it again. He's crippled. Go in for the kill. Put this joker out of his misery. Thanks for playing, jerk. I out thought ya and I out fought ya.

And there you are. Breathing heavy. Slightly dazed. Victorious. Alone.

When you fight monsters you must use monstrous tactics to have a chance to win. How do you come back to civilized society after that? How can you heed Nietzsche's warning and fight monsters without becoming one? How do you keep your humanity and any sense of grace after going down that rabbit hole? Many do not.

THE COST TO BE THE BOSS

"All truth passes through three stages. First it is ridiculed. Second it is violently opposed. Third, it is accepted as being self evident."
—Arthur Schopenhauer

Here's the good news, getting punched in the face is just part of the process. When you first step onto the stage as a dealmaker, people will view you as pup and not take you seriously. Then when you start to gain some traction, your competitors will start to get nervous, agitated. Then when you seem like a threat you will become a target. People will start trying to take you out. Ironically, this is actually a good thing. If people come at you that hard, you are likely rising from a mere pig, who should not be wrestled, to a worthy opponent, who should be taken seriously. With a little luck you might even become hated, a prodigious sign of respect. The great talent manager and producer Bernie Brillstein actually titled his fantastic autobiography, in part, *You're No One in Hollywood Unless Someone Wants You Dead*. Bernie was right. Don't take it personally if people despise you; it probably means that you're on to something.

Survive the onslaught of hazing and perhaps pull off an upset or two. Your industry is slowly but surely learning that you are not going anywhere. You will not be blown out of the biz. Ultimately, the community accepts your worthiness as a dealmaker to be self-evident. Of course you're great, obviously! Everyone knows that. Everyone also conveniently forgets how they ridiculed and violently opposed your ascension. No matter. You still fight, but now the stakes are higher and competitors tread with greater caution. You've earned your stripes and paid the cost to be the boss. Pain is temporary, victory is eternal.

FORBEARANCE

"Like many brilliant men he had grown up dead cold . . . with the total rejection common to those of extraordinary mental powers . . . Instead of being a son-of-a-bitch as most of them are he looked around at the barrenness that was left and said to himself 'This will never do.' And so he learned tolerance, kindness, forbearance, and even affection like lessons."
—F. Scott Fitzgerald/The Love of the Last Tycoon

F. Scott Fitzgerald had moved to Hollywood to try his hand at screenwriting in the 1930s. He had gone from writing *The Great Gatsby* to writing short stories and screenplays for MGM without much success. He was drinking heavily, had serious financial difficulties and was estranged from his mercurial spouse, Zelda, who was living in various mental institutions on the East Coast. *The Love of the Last Tycoon* was his final novel. He died before it was completed. The main character is studio wunderkind, Monroe Stahr, whom the passage above is about. Fitzgerald based the character on MGM's "Boy Wonder," Irving Thalberg, one of the most successful and revered film producers in the history of Hollywood. Through Fitzgerald's characterization of Monroe Stahr, you can feel his adoration for Thalberg.

I keep a copy of *The Love of The Last Tycoon* next to my desk. When I'm feeling punch drunk or overwhelmed by the monsters I'm currently fighting, I read the part I quoted above. For me the key word in the passage is "forbearance," defined precisely as "patient self-control; restraint and tolerance."

How can you heed Nietzsche's warning and fight monsters without becoming one? In a word, forbearance. Monsters are incapable of practicing forbearance. Like in the famous fable of the scorpion and the frog. The kind frog allows the scorpion to ride on his back, to paddle him safely to the other side of a river. Midway through, the scorpion stings the frog, dooming them both to drown. As he is sinking, the frog asks the scorpion, "Why did you sting me? Now we both will die?" The scorpion replies, "Because, I'm a scorpion." Even though it was completely counter to his own self-interest, the scorpion was incapable of exercising forbearance. Stinging the frog was an exercise of monstrous impulse, an unreasonable act lacking in dignity and self-control. Never let yourself become that scorpion. In the heat of a battle, no matter how vicious, you must never lose your ability to practice restraint when reason dictates to do so.

> *"Next to knowing when to seize an opportunity, the most important thing in life is knowing when to forgo an advantage."*
> **—Benjamin Disraeli**

The legal definition of forbearance is "refraining from doing something that one has a legal right to do." Why would anyone practice forbearance? Why forgo an advantage? Is it because we're good people? No. It's because we're smart people. Critical thinking is the single best ability we have as a species. Humans dominate earth singularly because of our intellect. Apes are stronger. Horses are faster. Wolverines are more ferocious. Dogs are nicer. Three-toed sloths are way cooler. Mastering the art of forbearance allows us to maintain the ability to think critically under even the most demanding of circumstances. It is usually during these circumstances that clear-headedness is needed most. Forbearance allows us to transcend the petty animal impulses. Hate is replaced with empathy. Anger is replaced by pity.

Don't get me wrong, per the Power Punishment Paradigm, bad behavior is always met with punishment. But, this comes from a place of reason, in service of improving the terms of the transaction and self-defense. Why waste energy on pointless and unprofitable revenge against your enemies when that same energy can be used to make things better for yourself and your allies?

Be like Fitzgerald's Monroe Stahr. Survey the barrenness that surrounds you without letting it turn you into a "son-of-a-bitch." Internalize the virtue of forbearance to become elevated by the challenge of combat instead of debased by the horror of it.

SHELTER FROM THE STORM

"Perhaps love is like a resting place, a shelter from the storm"
—John Denver

You've read *The Dealmaker's Ten Commandments*. You're obviously bright, hard working and have great taste in literature. You will do well in business. You will make a good living. But will you make a good life? Dealmaking can be a hazardous and exhausting endeavor. You need downtime to rejuvenate your mind and spirit. Running on empty is romantic, but not sustainable. It prevents you from functioning at your peak capacity. You need to find or create a safe place to recharge those batteries and enjoy the spoils of victory. You need shelter from the storm.

TRANSITION

Finding an effective way to transition from your work environment to your personal environment is key. Trust me, I understand how difficult this can be. But, by hook or by crook, you must find a way to leave work at work if possible. The quality of your personal life is in direct proportion to your ability to be present and mindful at home. Put the smartphone away, your e-mails and social media updates will be there in the morning. I've found that having a middle activity between being engaged at work and being engaged at home is helpful. Perhaps you play a video game for 30 minutes or watch an episode of your favorite show. Watch out for leaning on substances to relax after work and make the transition. Mind you, I'm not above having a stiff martini after a particularly tough work day, but be careful. It's a hell of a tight rope to walk.

PHYSICAL OUTLET

Whether it's the treadmill at the gym or yoga at home or playing in the local basketball league, you need to have a physical outlet for your mental stress. It goes without saying, but being in better shape makes you more energetic, sharper and able to do better work.

MENTAL OUTLET

It is also imperative to have a healthy outlet for the mental stress and anxiety from the pressures of your professional life. This can be any combination of therapy, journaling, meditation or whatever is helpful to you. It is important that there is a constant release valve for your mental tension because it will build up.

LAUGH ON OCCASION

I love this quote from Peter Ustinov: *"It is our responsibilities, not ourselves, that we should take seriously."* Our job may be serious stuff, but we shouldn't take ourselves too seriously. Have a sense of humor. Everything is pretty ridiculous when you really think about it.

GET A LIFE

Finding shelter from the storm is really about getting a life outside of your career. I know that's harder than it sounds, especially for us Type-A lunatics. Learn to not equate the value of your work product with your value as a person. Your success as a professional is part of the calculus, but not all of it. Having a vibrant personal life with love, compassion, friendship and a little bit of adventure has value as well. Besides, you're going to need somewhere to spend all that money you're making as a big-time dealmaker.

INSIDER OUT

"I think you only really feel like an outsider if you've been an insider."
—Sade

My favorite film portrayal of a lawyer is hands-down Robert Duval's Tom Hagen in *The Godfather* and *The Godfather II.*[1] Hagen is consiglieri, a trusted lawyer and counselor to Don Vito, then Don Michael Corleone. He is privy to their deepest secrets, speaks fluent Italian and flawlessly executes the will of his Don, his client, his family. He is brother to Sonny, Fredo and Michael, but only in part. He is Irish and was taken in by the Corleone family after he ran away from his abusive, alcoholic father. Part of the family, but not. Powerful, but in constant danger of his power being revoked, which happens when Michael unceremoniously strips him of his position:

> **Tom Hagen:** Michael, why am I out?
> **Michael Corleone:** You're not a wartime *consigliere*, Tom. Things may get rough with the move we're trying.

---

1. This is my last *Godfather* reference, I pinky swear!

The brilliance of Duvall's performance is in the tension of his dutifully serving as counsel to his family while quietly longing to be more a part of his family. It's a subtle and heartbreaking undercurrent throughout the films. You can see it in his eyes.

One of the most challenging parts about being a lawyer, specifically, and representative, generally, is that you are an insider and outsider simultaneously. You are passionately vested in your client's interests but ultimately separate from them. And just like it was for Tom Hagen, it can be a taxing, melancholy affair.

An object is not supposed to exist in two different places at the same time. But, representatives do, because we must. We need to be distant to see the big picture, to be objective. We need to be close to understand what our client really wants, to know how they feel and to be able to support them through the dealmaking process. It feels weird, because it is. It is also necessary to do our job properly.

If you are a rep and you cease to be useful, you might be out just like Tom Hagen. You're part of the family, but you're also not part of the family. You can't begrudge your client; they are just doing what they perceive to be in their best interests. Maybe it is, maybe it isn't? Sometimes, it doesn't matter. It's just part of the game. Try not to take it personally. Better yet, cultivate or create or join a family of your own. Might come in handy when you need a break from dealmaking . . .

QUESTION FOR SELF-MASTERY

HAVE I CROSSED THE BRIDGE?

"You are permitted in time of grave danger to walk with the devil until you have crossed the bridge."

—**Bulgarian Proverb**

Look around, ask yourself, "Have I crossed the bridge?" Is the deal done? If not, knuckle up and keep swinging. But if so, then it's time to come back. It's OK. The danger has passed; you're safe. Yes, you walked with the devil. Did some ugly things. You had to. Wouldn't have made it across the bridge if you didn't. The enemy was merciless, the stakes were high, the combat brutal and ferocious. But, you've got the chops. Often outnumbered, but never outgunned. You're the

Bogey Man, Freddy Krueger, Nosferatu. You're what goes bump in the night, handing out ulcers like Santa hands out candy canes. Feared, not loved.

Breathe. The time for monstrosity has past. You have to come back. Back to your family, back to your friends. They miss you.

Breathe. Just breathe. It's over. You gave more than you got. It's done. It's good. Put it away. The time for walking with the devil has passed for now. You are no longer permitted to do so. Walking with the devil is intoxicating. He's great company. But get too close, and you get burned. Stay too long, and things get hazy. You can't find your way home. They need you there, not as a deal-maker though. Your kid needs a parent; your mate needs a lover; your mother needs her child. And you need to find your way back home, to remember who you were before you crossed that damn bridge. It's symbiotic like that. Take their hands, they remember and long to show you the way.

> *"We shall not cease from exploration*
> *And at the end of all our exploring*
> *Will be to arrive where we started*
> *And know the place for the first time."*
>
> —T.S. Eliot

At the end of our journey, we will be where we began and know it for the first time.

OUR JOURNEY THUS FAR . . .

DEALMAKER'S COMMANDMENT I: IT IS BETTER TO BE FEARED THAN LOVED.

Being feared is more useful and reliable than being loved.

DEALMAKER'S COMMANDMENT II: POWER LEADS; REASON FOLLOWS.

Power, not reason, drives the outcome of a transaction.

DEALMAKER'S COMMANDMENT III: EVERYONE IS ON THE SAME SIDE . . . THEIR OWN.

Parties are motivated by and can be predicted to behave in accordance with their perceived best self-interest.

DEALMAKER'S COMMANDMENT IV: THINGS ARE PRECISELY AS THEY SEEM.

All manner of irrational and emotional impulses must be shaved away to objectively analyze the battlefield.

DEALMAKER'S COMMANDMENT V: NO PIG WRESTLING.

Combat is honor. Choose your enemies and battles wisely. If combat is thrust upon you, choose to define your enemy and the conditions for victory.

DEALMAKER'S COMMANDMENT VI: TAKE YES FOR YES, MAYBE FOR YES AND NO FOR MAYBE.

Dealmaking is a dance whose basic steps are: offer, counter, close. Conduct the tempo and tune to your advantage.

DEALMAKER'S COMMANDMENT VII: DO IT, DELETE IT, DELEGATE IT.

Time is the dealmaker's commodity. Set goals and create a time-management system to maximize the impact of your labor and resources.

DEALMAKER'S COMMANDMENT VIII: DON'T PANIC, STOP THE BLEEDING, DON'T COMPOUND THE ERROR.

Train yourself to calmly and effectively handle emergencies. Then, fix the problem, analyze the error and improve the algorithm.

DEALMAKER'S COMMANDMENT IX: BE A DEALMAKER, NOT A DEAL BREAKER

Dealmakers make deals. Know your role, get paid and remember your ABCs. Always be closing.

DEALMAKER'S COMMANDMENT X: HEED NIETZSCHE'S WARNING.

Don't allow fighting monsters to make you a monster. Heed Nietzsche's warning by internalizing the virtue of forbearance and finding shelter from the storm.

Congrats! You have learned them all! Applause, applause! You get a standing ovation. Time for the CURTAIN CALL!

CURTAIN CALL

"Say what you will about the Ten Commandments, you must always come back to the pleasant fact that there are only ten of them."

—H. L. MENCKEN

I'm going to miss you. Yeah, that's weird. I don't know you. But, I do know that you bought *The Dealmaker's Ten Commandments*, so I'm going to assume that you're pretty cool. Writing this book has felt like a conversation to me. A very one-sided conversation, but a conversation nonetheless. Feel free to continue the conversation by following me on Twitter @jeff_b_cohen or liking my Facebook page. www.facebook.com/ JeffBCohenEsq.

I very much appreciate you granting me the right to share my philosophy. If my experiences can help you achieve your goals and perhaps learn a bit about yourself along the way, well that's just about the best thing I can do with my life. I think about all the books I read when I was struggling and how helpful they were to me. They inspired me. They allowed me to bask in that exquisite sunlight of unmitigated intellectual freedom. They showed me that I wasn't alone, that I could be something greater. They gave me hope.

As I wrote at the beginning and now return to at the end: Success is life on your own terms. The Dealmaker's Ten Commandments have helped me successfully negotiate the terms of my life, and I sincerely hope they help you successfully negotiate the terms of yours.

You've got this. Give 'em hell!

SUGGESTED READING

Bacon, F. (1627). *The Essays of Sir Francis Bacon.*

Blanchard, K. (2003). *The One Minute Manager.*

Brillstein, B. (2008). *Where Did I Go Right?: You're No One in Hollywood Unless Someone Wants You Dead.*

Crowther, B. (2012). *Hollywood Rajah: The Life and Times of Louis B. Mayer.*

Ferriss, T. (2009). *The 4-Hour Workweek: Escape 9-5, Live Anywhere, and Join the New Rich.*

Fitzgerald, F. (1941). *The Love of the Last Tycoon.*

Hobbes, T. (2011). *Leviathan.*

King, T. (2000). *The Operator: David Geffen Builds, Buys, and Sells the New Hollywood.*

Lakein, A. (1989). *How to Get Control of Your Time and Your Life*

Laozi. (1900). *Tao Te Ching.*

Linson, A. (1998). *A Pound of Flesh: Perilous Tales of How to Produce Movies in Hollywood.*

Machiavelli, N. (1984). *The Prince.*

Masters, K. (2001). *Keys to the Kingdom: The Rise of Michael Eisner and the Fall of Everybody Else.*

Matthews, C. (2009). *Life's a Campaign.*

McDougal, D. (2001). *The Last Mogul: Lew Wasserman, MCA, and the Hidden History of Hollywood.*

McGonigal K., Ph.D. (2013). *The Willpower Instinct: How Self-Control Works, Why It Matters, and What You Can Do to Get More of It.*

Mencken, H. (2003). *The Philosophy of Friedrich Nietzsche.*

Nietzsche, F. (1883). *Thus Spoke Zarathustra.*

Nietzsche, F. (1886). *Beyond Good and Evil.*

Rock, D. (2009). *Your Brain at Work: Strategies for Overcoming Distraction, Regaining Focus, and Working Smarter All Day Long.*

Schulberg, B. (1952). *What Makes Sammy Run?*

Spence, G. (1996). *How to Argue & Win Every Time: At Home, At Work, In Court, Everywhere, Everyday.*

Tzu, S. (2010). *The Art of War.*

Vieira, M. (2009). *Irving Thalberg: Boy Wonder to Producer Prince.*

Weatherford, J. (2005). *Genghis Khan and the Making of the Modern World.*

Webster, M. (1992). *The Merriam-Webster Dictionary of Quotations.*

ACKNOWLEDGMENTS

Thanks to all of my clients for honoring me with their trust. It is a beautiful and sacred responsibility which I treasure.

Thanks to Niccolò Machiavelli for having the guts to speak his truth without quarter. Those dark words gave my life illumination when I needed it most.

My gratitude to Richard Donner and Lauren Shuler-Donner is immeasurable. Not only were Dick and Lauren remarkably kind to me when things were rough, they have served as continuous examples of what wonders people can accomplish with lives lived extraordinarily.

Thanks to Jon Malysiak for being such a supportive, talented editor and the good folks at the American Bar Association/Ankerwycke for providing me with an opportunity to share my philosophy. If Jon didn't reach out to me, this book would not exist. I can't thank him enough. Thanks to my pal and colleague Bradley Garrett, Esq. for being a fantastic attorney and this dealmaker's Dealmaker. Thanks to Ken Gillett and his team at Target Digital Marketing for their excellent work on the PR front. Thanks to Daniel Greenberg and Tim Wojcik at Levine Greenberg Rostan Literary Agency for their great work regarding the audiobook.

Thanks so much to the erudite, witty and wise Steven Gaydos for writing a beautiful foreword. Thanks to the eternally philanthropic, savvy and discerning Brian Gott for his fantastic words in support of *The Dealmaker's Commandments*. Thanks to the charismatic, talented and insightful Terry City for his support of the book as well.

Thanks to Mama Cohen for loving me infinitely, taking me on all those auditions and coming to every one of my football games. Raising me and Eydie as a single mother was a herculean task of which I stand in constant awe. I hope you are proud of me and my book. Please brag to your friends till their ears bleed. That's why I wrote this damn thing. Love you Mom!

Thanks to Eydie for being a fantastic sister, amazing writer, mother par excellence and a great friend. Thanks to Ben for being the best bra in-law an Irish Jew from the Valley could wish for. Thanks to Violet, Ruby and Goldie for being such awesome nieces. You are wonderful little humans and I am so fortunate to be your Uncle. I can't wait to see all the great things you will accomplish.

Thanks to Jackie for being a splendiferous co-pilot, making me laugh and holding my hand throughout this challenging adventure.

Thanks to Leslie for saying I'm a good boss, when she is really my boss, and a damn fantastic one at that. Thanks to Heather for her invaluable assistance with *The Dealmaker's Commandments*. Thanks to Jonathan, Jennifer and Marize for fostering such a dynamic environment at the firm. Thanks to Natasha for being this advocate's advocate. Thanks to Michelle, Peter C, Kate, Dawn, Peter D, Donna and all the great people at *Variety* for officially anointing me "Dealmaker." It's the Bar Mitzvah I never had.

Thanks to Theresa, Larry and Courtney for allowing me to be a part of their beautiful family. Thanks to Rich and Michele for being so damn adorable together. Thanks to Ryan for the endless hours of Nintendo growing up. Thanks to Ian for taking the leap and being my first client ever. Thanks to Danielle for being so kind. Thanks to Matt for bringing the wisdom of Scarface into my life. Thanks to Hugh for co-founding our gang, The Unstoppables. Thanks to Alonso for being hilarious and fearless. Thanks to Julia for the friendship and knowledge.

Thanks to Taft High, UC Berkeley (GO BEARS!), UCLA Law and the great public school system of California for giving me a chance to create a better life for myself. I firmly believe that in our democracy, public education remains the best mechanism for social mobility.

Thanks to Ned and Jason for showing me the ropes. Thanks to Dave for teaching me what it means to be a vet. Thanks to Dan for letting me bug him in his office with silly show biz schemes far too often. I wish he was around to read my book, I hope he would have liked it.

Above all, I'd like to thank my Bubbe for loving me unconditionally, being the best cook the world has ever seen and never letting me win at Monopoly. She departed our mortal plane decades ago, but wanders through my heart each day. With the memory of her, I am never alone. I'm eternally grateful for that.

Last and certainly least, to all of those who planted their best haymaker on my mug when I was vulnerable and afraid: as Jake LaMotta whispered to "Sugar" Ray Robinson in *Raging Bull*, "*You never got me down Ray . . . you never got me down.*"